"In this treasure of a book, Zachary Yonko combines exegetical acumen with a poet's eye to open new windows of understanding into the sixty-six books of the Bible. There is a simple, authentic, and elegant beauty in his poetry that leads readers to an experience Scripture's own beauty. These poems can serve as a wonderful companion for personal Bible study and daily devotion. They have nourished my soul, and they will nourish yours as well!"

—L. DANIEL HAWK, Professor of Old Testament and Hebrew, Ashland Theological Seminary

"Here you find true sincerity, dynamic faith, and poetic craftsmanship. Engagement with the reader matters as much to Yonko as engagement with the biblical texts. It is a masterful invitation to share his gifted interpretations. He writes about the Gospel of John, 'I feel like I've been drawn into a world that's both vast and intimate.' That is how I felt while reading this book. Zachary Yonko, thank you for writing it."

—ROBERT M. RANDOLPH, Professor Emeritus, Texas State University

"In *Sixty-Six Reveries*, Yonko accepts one of the most joyful invitations given to us by our Creator, to dance a tango with the word through verse, spinning out sixty-six new creations in response. These poems are intimate considerations of ancient lives and stories, brought into the bright spirit and cadence of Zac's particular voice and faith."

—SARAH M. WELLS, author of *Ordinary Time: Meditations from the In-Between*

"Do you like poetry? I have no experience reflecting on poetry outside of Scripture, but *Sixty-Six Reveries* is a rewarding and insightful reflection on God's word. Zac 'closes' each book and letter, giving us such a thought-provoking journey through God's word! Your musings and insight are refreshing for my own contemplations—thanks, brother!"

—TONY WEBB, Founder, Vision USA Church Planting

Sixty-Six Reveries

Sixty-Six Reveries

A Poet's Walk Through the Field of Scripture

ZACHARY YONKO

RESOURCE *Publications* • Eugene, Oregon

SIXTY-SIX REVERIES
A Poet's Walk Through the Field of Scripture

Copyright © 2025 Zachary Yonko. All rights reserved. Except for brief quotations in critical publications or reviews, no part of this book may be reproduced in any manner without prior written permission from the publisher. Write: Permissions, Wipf and Stock Publishers, 199 W. 8th Ave., Suite 3, Eugene, OR 97401.

Resource Publications
An Imprint of Wipf and Stock Publishers
199 W. 8th Ave., Suite 3
Eugene, OR 97401

www.wipfandstock.com

PAPERBACK ISBN: 979-8-3852-4713-4
HARDCOVER ISBN: 979-8-3852-4714-1
EBOOK ISBN: 979-8-3852-4715-8

04/08/25

THE HOLY BIBLE, NEW INTERNATIONAL VERSION®, NIV® Copyright © 1973, 1978, 1984, 2011 by Biblica, Inc.® Used by permission. All rights reserved worldwide.

This book is dedicated in loving memory of my grandmother, Betty J. (Carcella) Saiani—the most loving person I have ever met. Her kindness, wisdom, and unwavering love continue to inspire me every day.

Contents

Acknowledgments | xi
Introduction | xiii

PART 1 | THE OLD TESTAMENT

In the Beginning, a Pause | 3
Crossing | 5
Instructions for Holiness | 6
Counting the Days | 7
Threshold | 8
Stepping In | 9
A Time Without Kings | 11
Where You Go | 12
The Boy Who Listened | 13
The Weight of a Crown | 14
Fire and Silence | 16
The Fall | 18
The Names We Carry | 20
The Rise and the Ruin | 22
The Return | 24
The Walls We Build | 26
The Silence of Providence | 28

CONTENTS

The Question | 30
The Songs We Sing | 32
The Wisdom | 34
The Search | 36
The Song | 38
The Voice in the Wilderness | 40
The Heart of the Prophet | 42
The Mourning | 44
The Vision | 46
The Dreams | 48
The Unfaithful | 50
The Locusts | 52
The Shepherd's Voice | 55
The Little Book | 57
The Reluctant Prophet | 59
The Scales of Justice | 62
The End of Nineveh | 65
The Complaint | 68
The Day of the Lord | 71
The Rebuilding | 73
The Dreamer's Call | 75
The Last Word | 78

PART 2 | THE NEW TESTAMENT

The Genealogy | 83
The Immediate | 86
The Laughter of Angels | 89
In the Beginning Was the Word | 92
The Ongoing | 96
The Letter | 100

CONTENTS

The Letter to the Divided | 103
The Letter of Tears | 107
The Letter That Burns | 111
The Letter to the Ones Who Are Already Seated | 115
The Letter from the Jailhouse | 120
Letter to the Disconnected | 124
The Letter of Joy from the Other Side | 129
The Letter of Steadying Hands | 134
Pastoral Epistle with a Cup of Coffee | 138
Final Instructions Before Winter | 143
How to Pastor an Island | 145
Paul, the Holy Guilt-Tripper | 147
A Letter Without a Name | 149
James Doesn't Mess Around | 151
Peter Writes to the Scattered | 153
Peter's Last Words | 155
John, the Old Man, Writes | 157
John Keeps It Short | 159
John, One More Time | 161
Jude's One Last Warning | 163
Revelation: The Last Vision | 165

Epilogue | 169
Index of Verses Referenced | 171

Acknowledgments

POETRY DOES NOT BLOOM in a vacuum. It is shaped by voices—by those who hand us our first books, who scribble encouragement in the margins, who sit across from us in coffee shops and let us ramble about words and wonder. This book is filled with fingerprints, and I want to take a moment to trace them back to the hands that have shaped me.

To my English teachers at Westmont Hilltop High School: Thank you for cracking open the door to creative writing and letting the light spill in. You gave me the tools to see the world in metaphor, and I have not stopped looking since.

To the English professors at Waynesburg University: You did far more than teach literature. You nurtured a twenty-year-old trying to discern God's calling through the arts, and in doing so, you left an imprint on every stanza I write. That department is special, a kind of home for wandering minds and restless pens. I could not have done this without you.

To my professors at Ashland Theological Seminary: You gave me the language and framework to wrestle with Scripture both thoughtfully and creatively. You showed me that sacred text and poetic text are not so different—they both ask us to listen closely, to sit with mystery, to lean in.

To my family and friends: Thank you for always being my first readers, my sounding boards, the ones who endure my "What do you think of this?" messages at all hours. I have rarely written anything without turning to you.

Acknowledgments

And finally, to my wife, Tessa, my biggest supporter, my steady place: This book was a journey, and you never stop walking with me. In every poem I ever write, you are there. This book, like my life, carries your love in its margins.

If we have spent any time together, even briefly, I can promise you this: some part of you is in these pages. Your fingerprints are here, pressed between the lines. Thank you for being part of the reverie.

Introduction

THIS COLLECTION OF POEMS was birthed from a journey through the pages of the Bible, a journey that took me approximately two and a half years to complete. After reading each book, I felt compelled to capture my reflections in verse—moments of humor, challenge, and encouragement. The poems serve as my personal response to the texts, where I sought not only to understand the profound depth of the Scripture but also to find my own connection to its messages. From the creation narrative in Genesis to the apocalyptic imagery of Revelation, each poem represents a moment of pause, a breath after reading, as I tried to distill the essence of each book's message into words that resonated deeply with my own life and faith.

As I wrote these poems, I found myself dancing between reverence and levity, allowing both the weight of Scripture and the lightness of reflection to coexist. My hope is that these poems speak to you in much the same way that the books of the Bible have spoken to me. Each verse and each letter found its place in these pages, and I invite you to pause, reflect, and perhaps even smile as you read. Just as the Bible holds layers of meaning waiting to be discovered, so too do these poems hold moments of insight, humor, and reflection. May they accompany you as you engage with the Scriptures and see the divine in both the serious and the unexpected.

Part 1

The Old Testament

IN THE BEGINNING, A PAUSE

I imagine God
sitting at a desk,
a blank sheet of light before Him,
tapping His fingers on the edge of eternity,
wondering where to begin.
Not that He is indecisive—
only that He enjoys a good opening line.
Something with weight.
Something that echoes when read aloud.
Something that makes the void sit up straight.
He exhales, and light spills everywhere,
like an ink bottle knocked over,
filling in the deep creases of space
until it all makes sense.
Then the world rolls out like a rug,
oceans smoothing themselves into place,
trees stretching their green fingers skyward,
and the animals, unaware
of the quiet significance of their arrival,
shake off the dust and wander forward.
And finally, a man.
Then a woman.
Then a bite, a curse,
a door swinging shut behind them.
I close the book
and sit for a moment,

watching the light shift in the room,
wondering what it was like
to be the first pair of bare feet
touching the cool morning of the world.

CROSSING

I think of them often,
not in the grand, golden light of Charlton Heston,
not with staffs raised high or seas splitting like theater curtains,
but in the smaller moments—
when the first sandal pressed into the wet sand
and someone hesitated,
wondering if the walls of water would hold,
if this was truly escape
or just another trick of the desert.
I think of the children,
too young to know the weight of it all,
splashing in puddles left by history,
while their parents whispered names of plagues
as if afraid they might follow.
And Moses,
somewhere near the front,
not looking back—
not daring to—
knowing that if he did,
he might see the dust rising,
the sound of hoofbeats swallowed by the wind.
I close the book,
and in the quiet,
I wonder if faith is nothing more
than stepping forward
before the path is clear.

INSTRUCTIONS FOR HOLINESS

It begins like a cookbook,
a long, careful list of what to bring,
what to burn,
what to wave before the Lord
as if He enjoys the aroma of grilled obedience.
There are rules for skin,
for fabric,
for birds fallen from the sky,
for the priest inspecting the slow geography of disease.
Even mildew has its moment in the sacred text.
I imagine the Israelites nodding,
trying to memorize the weight of each command,
marking the margins of their minds—
No mixed threads, no pork, no blemished offerings.
A life of watchfulness,
a holiness measured in careful steps.
And yet, nestled between the warnings,
a whisper of something softer:
Love your neighbor as yourself.
As if God knew
we'd remember the blood and fire,
but forget the simplest law of all.
I close the book,
not sure if I would have kept up,
if I would have remembered
which sins require a lamb
and which only ask for my heart.

COUNTING THE DAYS

It begins with a census,
a roll call in the wilderness,
each name a pebble in the great river of Israel,
each number a step toward the promise
or a reminder of how far they still have to go.
Forty years is a long time
to wander the same stretch of dust,
to wake up every morning to yesterday's scenery,
to keep walking even when you forget
what you're walking toward.
The people grumble—
of course they do.
Manna again?
More rules, more marching,
more wondering if they'll ever stop
long enough to build something that lasts.
I imagine them losing track of time,
counting their days
the way I count steps on a staircase,
as if the act of numbering
will make the journey feel smaller.
I close the book,
wondering if faith is sometimes
just the discipline of putting one foot
in front of the other,
trusting that the horizon
isn't playing tricks on you.

THRESHOLD

Moses stands at the edge of the story,
a man with more years behind him than ahead,
his voice worn smooth like river stones
from decades of telling them what God wants.
He repeats himself—
not because they weren't listening,
but because they forget.
Because we all forget.
He tells them again about Egypt,
about manna, about fire on the mountain,
about laws carved into stone and into life,
about a God who walks with them,
even when they don't notice the footprints.
But he knows—
he won't cross the river.
He will only watch as they go,
his hands empty,
his work complete.
I close the book,
thinking of the moments before change,
the weight of a threshold beneath your feet,
and the voices behind you
reminding you who you are.

STEPPING IN

It begins with a river,
wide and impatient,
water curling around the ankles
of priests who have been told—just step in.
The people watch,
holding their breath,
waiting to see if the stories
their parents told them were true,
if this God still splits waters
and makes a way where there isn't one.
Then the march,
circling Jericho like a question,
footsteps pressed into dust,
horns cutting the silence,
as if the walls could be unraveled
by sound alone.
And when they fall—
stone by stone,
fear by fear—
they walk forward,
not just into a city,
but into the promise
that led them here.
I close the book,
wondering how many walls
I have tried to tear down with my own hands

instead of waiting
for the sound of surrender.

A TIME WITHOUT KINGS

It is the age of wild stories,
of foxes with burning tails,
of tent pegs driven through skulls,
of a man pulling down a temple with his last breath.
The people wander in circles,
not through the wilderness this time,
but through their own mistakes—
forgetting God,
crying out for help,
being rescued,
then forgetting all over again.
The judges rise like sudden storms—
Deborah, wise beneath her palm tree,
Gideon, hiding in a winepress,
Samson, blinded but still dangerous.
Each one called from the ordinary,
each one asked to hold the line
until the people forget again.
I close the book,
seeing too much of myself in its pages,
wondering how many times
I have been rescued
only to run right back
into the arms of my ruin.

WHERE YOU GO

The emptiness—
a husband buried,
two sons gone,
a woman standing at the border
between what was and what's left.
Naomi tells Ruth to turn back,
to find a life that makes sense,
but Ruth holds on,
words spilling from her like a vow:
Where you go, I will go.
So they walk together,
two widows leaning into the wind,
feet tracing the road to Bethlehem,
where barley bends in the fields
and a quiet kindness waits
in the shape of a man named Boaz.
The story does not split seas
or summon fire from heaven—
it simply shows two women,
choosing love over fear,
faithfulness over ease,
a slow redemption unfolding
in the hush of harvest.
I close the book,
thinking of the weight of small choices,
how a single yes
can carry us all the way home.

THE BOY WHO LISTENED

In the hush of the temple,
a boy curled beneath the weight of sleep,
until a voice—soft, insistent—
threads through the dark:
Samuel, Samuel.
He runs to Eli,
blinking in the lamplight,
certain that wisdom must sound like an old man's voice,
but Eli waves him off—
Go back to sleep.
Again, the call.
Again, the running.
Again, the weary priest's sigh.
Then finally—
Speak, Lord, for your servant is listening.
And just like that,
the boy becomes a prophet,
ears tuned to the frequency of heaven,
his life stitched into the rise and fall
of a king's troubled reign.
I close the book,
wondering how often I mistake
God's whisper for a dream,
how many times I have risen,
only to run in the wrong direction.

THE WEIGHT OF A CROWN

There was a throne,
not empty, but waiting—
a promise made long ago
to a shepherd boy
who only ever wanted to hold a harp.
David takes the seat,
but kingship is heavier than he thought,
heavier than a sling in the valley,
heavier than running from Saul,
heavier than the guilt
that lingers in the shadow of a rooftop.
He wins wars,
writes psalms,
loves recklessly,
sins just as recklessly,
then learns that power
is not the same as peace.
The sword never leaves his house.
Sons rise against him.
Friends betray him.
And still, God calls him a man after His own heart,
as if broken things
can still belong to Him.
I close the book,
thinking of the crowns we chase,
the ways we fall,

and the mercy that finds us
even then.

FIRE AND SILENCE

Hello Solomon,
wise enough to ask for wisdom,
building a temple so grand
that even the stones seem to hum with holiness.
For a while, all is gold and glory,
God's presence thick as cloud in the air.
But soon, the kingdom splinters,
the throne passing from hand to unsteady hand,
kings rising and falling
like waves against the shore.
And then Elijah—
standing alone on Mount Carmel,
mocking prophets who cut themselves
for a god who will not answer.
Then fire,
fierce and bright,
devouring the altar in a single breath,
as if to say, *I am still here.*
Yet later, in a cave,
Elijah learns what power really sounds like—
not in wind,
not in earthquake,
not in fire,
but in a whisper,
so quiet he has to lean in to hear it.
I close the book,

wondering how often I look for God
in the spectacle,
when all along,
He is speaking softly,
waiting for me to listen.

THE FALL

I can see a prophet departing—
Elijah lifted into the sky,
his cloak tumbling down like a farewell,
while Elisha stands below,
blinking at the sudden emptiness.
The miracles continue,
water healed, oil multiplied,
a boy raised from death
just to prove God is still watching.
But the kings—
oh, the kings.
One after another,
some wicked, some worse,
a few who try to turn back
but find the road too steep.
The kingdom cracks,
first Israel, then Judah,
walls torn down,
temple burned,
God's people led away in chains,
their songs caught in their throats
as they stare at the rivers of Babylon.
I close the book,
feeling the weight of endings,
the way we build,
the way we ruin,

the way God waits,
even when we walk away.

THE NAMES WE CARRY

I used to find this list boring—
name after name,
generation upon generation,
as if history itself is being whispered
from the dust of the earth.
Adam, Seth, Noah,
Abraham, Isaac, Jacob,
David, Solomon—
each a link in the long chain
of promise and failure,
of mercy laced through bloodlines.
Then the story retold,
not with scandal,
not with shadows,
but with glory sharpened at the edges—
David the king,
the dreamer of temples,
the singer of psalms,
his wars counted like sacred steps
toward something greater.
It is less about what went wrong
and more about what was meant to be,
as if to remind us
that even in the ruins,
God is still building.
I close the book,

wondering how my own name
might be written—
not for what I have lost,
but for what grace
has chosen to remember.

THE RISE AND THE RUIN

It begins with Solomon,
bathed in gold and wisdom,
lifting a temple so radiant
that even heaven seems to lean in.
The priests cannot stand,
the cloud is too thick,
the presence of God settling like a weight
too holy to bear.
For a moment,
it seems the story might hold,
that the people might finally stay faithful,
that the kingdom might last.
But then,
pride seeps through the cracks.
Kings falter, hearts wander,
altars are built to gods
who do not listen.
Prophets cry out like men in the wilderness,
but their voices are drowned
by the sound of swords unsheathing.
Until, at last,
the walls collapse,
the temple burns,
and the people are led away—
exiled, scattered,
turning back only as their sorrow deepens.

Yet even in the ashes,
a promise lingers,
a remnant remains,
and the story is not over.
I close the book,
wondering how many times
we must break
before we finally return.

THE RETURN

Where is that scroll,
dusty and worn,
but still breathing life
into hearts long buried under ruins?
A king's decree,
a promise forgotten by time,
but remembered by God.
The people return—
not as conquerors,
but as survivors,
carrying with them the weight of the years
and the hope of rebuilding.
Their hands, once empty,
now hold stones
and plans for a temple
that will never be as grand as the one they lost.
Ezra arrives with the law,
unfurling it like a banner,
his voice steady as the winds of history,
calling the people back to the rhythms
they had forgotten.
The temple rises,
not in the splendor of Solomon,
but in the quiet faith of those
who still remember what it means
to be chosen.

I close the book,
thinking of the things we rebuild
after the fire has passed,
and wondering if God is more
in the rubble we gather
than in the glory we once knew.

THE WALLS WE BUILD

I hear the report,
a broken city,
its gates burned to ash,
its walls crumbled like forgotten dreams.
Nehemiah's heart aches,
but his hands are steady,
his resolve as solid as stone.
He returns to Jerusalem,
not with the sword,
but with a shovel,
gathering the weary
to rebuild what was lost—
one brick at a time,
one prayer at a time,
one enemy silenced by the work
of faithful hands.
The walls rise,
slowly, steadily,
each stone a defiance
against the years of exile.
But it is not just the walls
that need rebuilding—
it is the people.
Their hearts, scattered by the winds of oppression,
must be gathered again
under the banner of God's law.

I close the book,
thinking of the walls we build
around our own hearts, no our souls—
how many cracks go unnoticed
until we stop and hear one another.

THE SILENCE OF PROVIDENCE

Joyous feast,
bright with wine and whispered secrets,
a queen discarded,
a kingdom on the edge of ruin.
Esther enters the story
not with a cry for help,
but with a quiet obedience,
a beauty that hides more
than the eye can see.
The king does not call her,
but she steps forward,
uninvited, unbidden—
a gamble with her life,
and yet, somehow,
she is crowned.
Haman plots,
evil woven into his every word,
his plan set to crush an entire people.
But in the shadows,
something moves—
a sleepless night,
a forgotten story,
a king who remembers
that a man named Mordecai
once saved his life.

There is no mention of God's name,
but His hand is on every turn,
every choice made in the quiet
and in the dark,
in the folds of a royal gown,
in the ink of a decree,
in the heart of a woman
who dares to speak.
I close the book,
wondering how many times
we fail to see God in the silence,
how His presence is woven
into the quiet acts of courage,
even when we don't say His name.

THE QUESTION

Do you know this man?
so righteous that even the heavens notice,
his days full of blessings
like rain on dry soil,
his heart untouched by bitterness,
his wealth a sign of God's favor.
Then the storm comes—
unexpected, ruthless—
and Job,
stripped of everything,
sits in ashes,
scraping his wounds with broken pottery,
his heart a labyrinth of grief and rage.
His friends arrive,
silent at first,
then speaking words that ache more
than the sores on his body.
They claim to know why it all happened,
as if God's will fits neatly into their theories,
as if suffering has an explanation
we can always find,
if we're clever enough.
Job demands an answer,
his voice shaking the heavens.

He questions,
he rages,
he dares to ask
the question that doesn't seem allowed—
Why?
And in the end,
God speaks—
but not with the neat answers Job expected,
not with a why,
but with a whirlwind of what—
What is the foundation of the world?
What holds the stars in place?
What can measure the depths of the sea?
And in the silence that follows,
Job finds himself small
and yet deeply known.
I close the book,
wondering if sometimes
God's answer to my suffering
is simply His presence,
not in explanations,
but in the mystery of the question.

THE SONGS WE SING

This song begins with a cry—
a shout from the heart,
a plea for rescue,
a hymn to the One
who never seems to answer
the way we expect.
The poet sings,
his words dancing like fire
and sinking like stones,
lifting the soul one moment,
dragging it down the next—
for the psalms are nothing
if not honest.
There's joy,
there's sorrow,
there's vengeance,
there's peace,
and in the middle,
there's a question—
Why, God, do you let the wicked prosper?
The psalmist writes
with a quill dipped in emotion,
his heart laid bare like a scroll
unfurled in the wind—
and we read,
and we sing,
and we do the same thing.

Yet isn't it ironic,
that the very words
we use to speak to God,
to ask, to plead, to praise,
are the same words
that come from the depths of our own need,
our own confusion,
our own struggle?
We turn them into poems,
songs to be sung,
and somehow,
they carry us closer
to the One we cannot understand.
I close the book,
wondering if poetry is just
another prayer dressed in rhythm,
and if perhaps,
the truest songs are the ones
we don't know how to sing
but must.

THE WISDOM

Was that a whisper of—
Listen, child, and I will show you the way,
a voice not shouting,
but soft, steady,
like the slow turn of a page
in a book you've always had but never read.
The proverbs come,
one after another,
a string of pearls,
each one a lesson wrapped in simplicity,
a rule, a warning, a promise—
The wise will inherit the earth,
but the foolish will fall,
as if it were that simple.
But is it?
The fool's path seems so wide,
so easy to follow,
so much like the one I want to walk,
and yet,
here is wisdom,
sitting like a beggar by the gate,
waiting for me to open my eyes.
Trust in the Lord with all your heart,
lean not on your own understanding,
and somehow,
in the quiet of the words,
I hear the answer I have been looking for.

And yet,
it never seems to work out as neatly
as the proverbs suggest.
The wise still stumble,
the fool still flourishes,
and I find myself asking,
What is the point of all this wisdom?
But the book keeps speaking—
a whisper, a nudge,
and I keep listening,
even when I don't want to.
I close the book,
wondering if the hardest thing about wisdom
is not learning it,
but living it.

THE SEARCH

Oh, that cry—
Meaningless! Meaningless!
A voice rising from the dust,
calling out to a world that spins on
while we chase after vapor,
grasping at things we cannot hold.
The Teacher watches—
with the eyes of a thousand lifetimes,
seeing the cycles of time
and the echo of human hearts
that never seem to learn.
The sun rises,
the wind blows,
the rivers flow to the sea,
but the sea is never full.
We build,
we plant,
we toil under the sun,
but nothing changes—
the rich die,
the wise grow old,
the fool laughs and drinks,
and in the end,
all are forgotten.
Yet still, the search continues—
for meaning in pleasure,

in work,
in wisdom,
in the fleeting moments that seem so sure,
until the dust settles,
and we are left with nothing
but the sound of our own questions.
And in the quiet,
the Teacher whispers—
Fear God and keep His commandments,
as if to say,
it is not in the things we grasp
that we find meaning,
but in the mystery of surrender,
in the quiet faith
that God holds all the answers
we will never understand.
I close the book,
thinking of the futility I often chase,
the moments that slip through my hands
and the peace found only in letting go.

THE SONG

Can this start with a kiss,
soft and lingering,
a breath held between two hearts,
a language older than words,
spoken in glances, in touch,
in the spaces where the world
cannot see?
The bride sings of love—
of the sweetness of the vineyard,
of the fragrance of the spice,
of a garden where the flowers bloom
for no one but the one she loves.
Her words are heavy with longing,
but light with joy,
as if the very air around her
was made to dance.
He responds—
his voice deep like the night,
the one who calls her his dove,
his perfect one,
as if her beauty could melt the world's coldest stone,
and her laughter could silence the thunder.
And yet—
it's just a song.

A song about love
that we sing,
or wish we could sing,
to one another,
to the world,
to God,
as if the melody could fill the spaces
we don't know how to say.
It's a song that's not really about love at all,
but about longing—
about the ache for something more,
something deeper,
something we can never fully touch,
but that always calls us,
always sings through us,
always pulls us into its rhythm,
even when we're not looking.
I close the book,
wondering if love is just the name
we give to the space between the notes,
the silence that makes the song
so much louder than the sound.

THE VOICE IN THE WILDERNESS

A loving cry—
a voice calling from the desert,
sharp, clear,
cutting through the noise
of a world too busy to listen.
Prepare the way of the Lord,
it says,
but who is ready for the road
to be made straight?
Isaiah speaks of judgment,
but it is a judgment wrapped in hope,
a promise that even the darkest nights
are not without their dawn.
He sees the world as it is—
broken, bleeding,
caught in a spiral of pride and sin—
but he also sees what it can be,
what it will be,
when the glory of the Lord
shines like the sun
on the earth that was made
to bear it.
The visions come—
seraphim and cherubim,
thrones and altars,
a King whose reign is not of this world,
but whose justice will pour down like rain.

Isaiah speaks of the suffering servant,
one who will bear the weight of it all,
who will carry the griefs
we were too proud to face.
And yet,
it's almost too much to bear—
this vision of a world that will never be
until it is,
a Kingdom that is already here
but not yet here,
a peace that passes understanding,
but only when the war is over.
I close the book,
wondering if this is the way of all prophets—
to speak what is,
but always point toward what will be,
to offer a glimpse of the light
before we've learned how to live in it.

THE HEART OF THE PROPHET

A nation unravels,
its heart turning cold,
stubborn like a stone
in the hands of a potter.
Jeremiah speaks to them,
his words trembling with grief,
a message not of hope,
but of the inevitable—
the destruction they've earned,
the price of their own waywardness.
He is called the weeping prophet,
for in his soul,
there is no joy to offer,
only sorrow for a people
who cannot hear the call to return.
His tears are the ink
of his prophecies,
written on the very walls of his heart.
They mock him,
stone him,
burn his words,
yet still, he speaks—
for he knows the truth,
even when it stings.
The heart of the people has become stone,
and there is no remedy but brokenness.

But in the midst of the ruin,
God promises something new,
a covenant not written on tablets,
but on the hearts of the people,
a law not outside them,
but inside them,
a law that will no longer be ignored,
because it will be their own.
Jeremiah's words are heavy,
the weight of them like chains,
but in the silence that follows,
there is a whisper—
a promise that even in the darkest days,
God will not abandon His people,
that the day will come
when they will return,
and their hearts will be whole again.
I close the book,
wondering if we, too,
are waiting for the day
when our own hearts are finally soft enough
to hear the voice we've been drowning out.

THE MOURNING

The city is silent now,
its walls crumbled like memories
of a life that was once full.
The streets, once crowded with joy,
are empty,
the air heavy with the smell of ash and sorrow.
The poet speaks in grief,
words spilling out like tears
too long held back,
crying out to God,
but finding no answer.
Why have you forsaken us?
is the question that lingers in the air,
unanswered,
the silence a weight that presses down
on the chest.
There are no bright songs here,
no songs of victory,
only the dirge of loss,
the ache of a people who were once whole
but are now scattered,
broken,
their joy lost in the rubble.
And yet, in the midst of the ruin,
there is a glimmer—
a faint hope that flickers,
like a candle struggling against the dark.

The poet remembers
that God's steadfast love
is still with them,
even in the desolation.
But it is a slow remembering,
a painful waiting,
as if the wounds must first be fully felt
before they can heal.
The poet's heart is raw,
but in the pain,
there is the whisper of redemption.
I close the book,
wondering if sometimes,
we must weep for the things we have lost
before we can begin to see
the small sparks of hope
that have always been there,
waiting to rise from the ashes.

THE VISION

There's a wheel within a wheel,
a fire that isn't fire
but still burns,
and four creatures with faces—
each one looking a little too much
like someone you'd prefer not to see
in your dreams.
Ezekiel's eyes are wide,
as wide as the sky he finds himself in,
and the voice that speaks from the storm
sounds a little too much
like a weather report
that warns you about things
you didn't know you should be afraid of.
The heavens are full of secrets,
whispers in the wind,
things that move in ways
you can't explain with a rational mind
or a decent thesaurus.
Son of man, stand up,
says the voice,
as if *standing* were optional
in a world where the ground doesn't quite hold you.
There's something about the dry bones,
scattered like forgotten laundry,
that seems oddly hopeful—
or maybe it's just the absurdity of it all.

You look at those bones,
ask them to rise,
and then, lo and behold—
they do!
And you're left wondering
if Ezekiel had a backup plan
for when the bones refused to cooperate.
The prophet doesn't get the luxury
of asking too many questions.
He's told to eat a scroll,
not the kind you find in a bakery,
but the kind that tastes like bitterness
and yet somehow satisfies.
He's told to lie on his side—
for a year—
and I can only imagine
the back pain he developed
and the confusion of his neighbors.
Oh, Ezekiel, what are you doing now?
And he answers with a straight face,
as if it were all normal.
I close the book,
wondering if the wheels within wheels
are just another metaphor
for trying to get through a Monday morning
without questioning everything,
or asking, "Why is this my life?"

THE DREAMS

There are dreams that make you sit up straight,
wide-eyed,
as if the very bed beneath you
might rise and start speaking in riddles.
Daniel has these kinds of dreams—
the ones that leave you scratching your head
and wondering if maybe the vegetables you ate
for dinner weren't as innocent as you thought.
There's a statue—
a giant one,
with a head of gold
and feet made of clay,
and somehow this is supposed to mean something.
Daniel interprets it, of course,
because when you're the guy who can't sleep
without a vision of the future
dancing in front of your eyes,
you become very popular at dinner parties.
Then there's the lion's den—
a situation I've never found myself in,
but if I had,
I'd probably be asking for a refund
on the whole "faithful servant" package.
But Daniel, with his cool, calm demeanor,
looks like he's just about to take a nap
while the lions pace,
their hungry eyes glittering.

He's either the bravest man on earth
or really good at pretending
he's not a little nervous.
The handwriting on the wall comes next—
as if things weren't mysterious enough—
and yet, even in the strangest of moments,
Daniel reads the writing
like it's just another Tuesday,
telling the king that his days are numbered,
which, if I were the king,
I'd take a lot more personally than I did.
And through it all,
there's a message—
somewhere between the dreams
and the lions,
the fire,
the kings,
and the handwriting—
that if you stay faithful,
even in the most absurd of situations,
you'll come out unscathed,
or at least with a very good story.
I close the book,
wondering if I, too,
might get a cryptic dream
about my future one day,
and whether or not I'd have the guts
to stand before a king
and say, *"Your days are numbered."*

THE UNFAITHFUL

God tells Hosea to marry a woman
who's already made up her mind
to break his heart.
This is the kind of relationship advice
that should come with a warning label.
Go, marry Gomer, God says,
as if Gomer's name didn't already sound
like trouble waiting to happen.
Hosea, the obedient prophet,
listens—
and he marries her.
Gomer runs off, of course,
like a child sneaking out of the house
to get a little extra sugar,
but she doesn't stop there—
she goes all the way,
wandering into a wilderness
of her own making,
leaving behind a trail of broken promises
and ruined trust.
And yet—
Hosea still loves her.
Still pursues her.
Still buys her back,
as if she were a possession
he can't bear to lose.

God watches it all—
like a parent,
sitting in the car,
watching their kid
make all the mistakes they warned them about,
but still hoping,
still loving,
still waiting for the moment
when the child will come running home.
There's something absurd in this love,
something that doesn't make sense,
because who loves like this?
Who gives second chances
to the ones who throw them away
without a second thought?
But then again,
maybe that's what love is—
the kind of love that doesn't measure
who's worthy of it,
but just pours out anyway,
even when the other person is busy
making all the wrong choices.
I close the book,
wondering if maybe I'm supposed to be more like Hosea—
willing to love
even when it hurts,
even when it doesn't make sense.
But I'm not sure I'm ready
to marry Gomer
just yet.

THE LOCUSTS

The locusts arrive
not in a single wave,
but as a parade—
marching over the fields
like they've been waiting for this moment
since the beginning of time.
They have no manners,
no sense of timing,
and certainly no respect for crops.
Joel sees them,
and he does what any prophet would do—
he starts calling for a fast.
He doesn't ask about the weather,
or if anyone is too busy to repent.
No, he just calls it—
like an unscheduled fire drill
where everyone suddenly remembers
how to panic.
The people are eating their bread
and suddenly,
the bread is gone—
the locusts have left them with nothing
but the taste of dust
and the bitter memory of what could have been.
And then Joel says the words
we all hope not to hear—
"Repent."

The kind of word that makes you
glance around to see if you can escape
through the nearest window.
But no one escapes—
not from the locusts,
not from the judgment,
not from the fact that sometimes
we are our own worst enemies.
And then, as if the locusts weren't enough,
Joel starts talking about the Spirit—
the kind of Spirit that comes
and fills your old bones
with fire and new dreams.
The kind of Spirit that makes you speak in languages
you've never learned
and prophesy about things
you've never seen.
But we don't talk about that part,
do we?
We prefer the locusts,
the destruction we can see and count,
the clear, obvious consequence
of our failures.
The Spirit?
That's the thing that waits until we're desperate
and then, in a moment,
gives us the courage to say the things
we were too afraid to say before.
I close the book,
wondering if it's time to stop waiting for the locusts
and start asking for the Spirit
instead—

and if, in doing so,
I might find myself
dreaming things
I didn't even know I could dream.

THE SHEPHERD'S VOICE

Amos doesn't belong here.
He's just a shepherd,
tending his flock like any other day,
when God taps him on the shoulder
and says, *Go. Speak.*
Amos looks around,
half expecting to see someone else behind him
who's far more qualified.
But no, it's him.
The sheep, oblivious, continue chewing.
So he walks,
a man in sandals and a robe
headed toward a city full of people
who think they're doing just fine.
They've got it all—
the crops, the wine, the power,
but somehow,
they've forgotten the thing
that made it all possible—
the quiet faithfulness of a God
they've been too busy to thank.
Amos doesn't mince words.
He's not into polite introductions.
He says, "You've been living large,
but you've been living wrong."
He starts calling out cities,
naming their sins like a shopping list—

a little here,
a little there,
as if God has been keeping score
all this time and now it's time to cash in.
And then—
just when you think Amos might be done—
he starts talking about justice.
He calls it like the waters of a flood—
the kind that sweeps through everything,
whether you've prepared for it or not.
He doesn't want nice words or half-measures.
He wants justice
the way a shepherd wants a lost sheep back.
But the people are not listening.
They're too busy with their festivals,
their feasts,
their luxury,
to hear the warning.
They look at Amos and wonder
why he didn't stay with his sheep,
where it's safe.
But Amos knows—
there's no safety in silence when the world's falling apart.
I close the book,
wondering how often we mistake comfort
for security,
how easily we ignore the things
that we know need fixing
because it's easier to pretend
we don't hear the shepherd's voice calling.

THE LITTLE BOOK

Obadiah is short.
In fact, it's so short,
you could almost miss it
if you blinked.
You could almost dismiss it,
thinking, *Surely this isn't important,*
with so many other prophets to choose from.
But here it is,
with one simple message—
Your time is up.
The Edomites,
those distant cousins,
sitting on the sidelines,
watching Israel fall,
laughing at their misfortune
like they're watching someone else's tragedy
from the safety of their couch.
Obadiah isn't interested in giving them a warm hug
or offering gentle advice.
No, he cuts straight to the point.
The day is coming,
he says,
and it will not be kind.
There's something almost comical
about how little it takes
for God to make a point.

One short prophecy,
and suddenly,
the Edomites are on notice.
All their pride,
all their high places,
all their cleverness
is nothing more than a house of cards
ready to fall.
The thing about Obadiah
is that he doesn't dwell on the fall.
It's not about how bad it will get for them,
but about how *right* it is.
The world doesn't turn on the wise or the powerful,
it turns on the justice
that God is constantly holding in balance.
I close the book,
realizing that sometimes the smallest messages
are the loudest,
and sometimes it's the people we least expect—
like Obadiah,
like the Edomites—
who end up with the biggest lessons.

THE RELUCTANT PROPHET

Jonah gets a call from God.
The kind of call you try to ignore,
like an alarm clock buzzing on a Sunday morning
when you know you should be up,
but you're too comfortable in the bed of your own stubbornness.
Go to Nineveh,
God says,
and Jonah, like any sane person,
looks around,
pretends he didn't hear it,
and heads in the opposite direction.
Nineveh? That's a long walk,
and frankly,
it doesn't sound like the kind of place
you'd want to vacation.
So Jonah boards a ship
and sails to Tarshish,
as far away as he can get.
But the sea has a mind of its own,
and it doesn't take long
before the storm shows up—
the kind of storm that leaves you wondering
if God has an awful sense of humor.
Jonah is thrown overboard,
swallowed by a fish—
a big fish,

not a metaphorical one,
but a real fish,
with real stomach acid
and a real sense of personal space violation.
Jonah spends three days
inside that fish,
probably regretting his life choices
and wondering if maybe
he should've just gone to Nineveh after all.
Finally, after the fish spits him out—
as fish tend to do—
Jonah trudges into the city,
a little worse for wear,
but still the messenger,
still the guy who's been sent
to tell people they've got it all wrong.
He's reluctant,
grumbling under his breath,
but he does it.
And you know what happens?
The people listen.
They repent.
They turn from their ways,
and Jonah, standing there,
arms crossed,
doesn't know whether to feel victorious
or annoyed.
It's a weird ending,
because Jonah's angry at God
for sparing Nineveh.
He wanted to see them get what they deserved,

but instead,
God shows mercy,
and Jonah's sitting there,
wondering why God's so good at forgiveness
and so bad at letting him have a petty moment.
I close the book,
laughing at the absurdity of it all,
thinking about how many times
I've tried to run from what I knew was right
only to find myself right back where I started,
wondering if I, too,
need a lesson in mercy.

THE SCALES OF JUSTICE

Micah stands on the edge,
looking out over a city
that thinks it's untouchable—
Jerusalem, dressed in its finest robes,
strutting around like a peacock
who forgot to look down.
"Listen!" he cries,
like a town crier in a world
too busy to stop.
The scales are tipping,
the balance is off,
and Micah's job is to point it out.
He doesn't hold back.
He calls out the rich,
the powerful,
the ones who've made deals with their consciences
and put their faith in gold,
not in justice.
But it's not just about the big guys.
No, Micah has a word for everyone.
The poor, the oppressed—
they've been forgotten too.
They've been tossed aside
like last season's fashion,
while the people at the top
sip their wine,

completely unaware of the cracks in the foundation
beneath their feet.
Micah doesn't have a lot of hope,
at least not in the immediate future.
He sees what's coming—
a day of reckoning,
where the rulers will be humbled,
and the people will be scattered,
like sheep without a shepherd.
The judgment is clear,
and yet—
in the middle of all this doom,
Micah whispers something else.
There will be a ruler,
a good one,
a humble one,
born not in a palace
but in the most unexpected place.
He won't wield power like the others.
He won't stand on a platform of privilege.
He'll be like the shepherds
who lead their flocks with care,
not with force.
It's a strange thing—
hope in the middle of despair.
Micah leaves us with a vision
not of what is,
but what could be,
if the people would listen,
if the scales of justice could be fixed,
if the rich could learn to give,

and the powerful could learn to serve.
I close the book,
wondering how often we try to build our towers,
only to forget
that true power doesn't come from the heights,
but from the depths
of humility and mercy.

THE END OF NINEVEH

Nahum stands on the outskirts,
watching the city from a distance,
his eyes narrowing at the smoke
rising from the streets of Nineveh.
He doesn't blink.
He doesn't waver.
This city, once mighty,
now sits like a beast
ready to be slain—
and Nahum, of all people,
is the one holding the sword.
He doesn't waste time with pleasantries.
It's over,
he says.
The mighty Assyrians,
those conquerors of the ancient world,
who once marched across nations
as though the earth was their playground,
will now feel the weight of their own cruelty
come crashing down.
Nahum doesn't make threats.
He simply declares facts.
The floodwaters are coming—
the kind of flood that doesn't ask permission,
the kind that sweeps through walls
and pulls down towers.

The soldiers will flee.
The riches will be plundered.
And Nineveh,
with all its pride and pomp,
will be reduced to rubble,
a cautionary tale for the ages.
It's strange to read.
A prophecy of judgment,
and yet Nahum delivers it
with the kind of satisfaction
you might feel
after seeing a bully finally get their due.
The Assyrians had terrorized for too long,
and now the scales of justice
have come for them.
But there's a little twist in all of this.
It's not just the fall of a city,
but a reminder of something deeper—
that cruelty,
arrogance,
and oppression
never win in the end.
They might seem powerful,
might seem invincible for a while,
but there's always a reckoning.
I close the book,
sitting with the weight of it all,
thinking how easy it is to forget
that every empire,
every ruler,
every force that seems untouchable,
is temporary.

Nahum reminds us:
the end always comes,
but it comes as both a warning
and a promise
of something more just,
something more enduring.

THE COMPLAINT

Habakkuk is frustrated.
And who can blame him?
He's watching the world spin wildly out of control,
and God—God, of all people—
seems to be standing idly by.
He starts with a question:
*How long, O Lord, will I cry for help
and you won't listen?*
It's a simple question,
but one that's been asked
since the dawn of time—
by the righteous,
by the oppressed,
by the disillusioned.
Habakkuk wants answers.
He doesn't just want to be patted on the back
and told to wait patiently.
He wants to know why things are happening
the way they are,
why the wicked prosper
while the faithful suffer.
God answers,
but not in the way Habakkuk expects.
God doesn't give him a neat little explanation
or tidy up the mess.

Instead, God says,
*I'm doing something you wouldn't believe
even if you were told.*
And then God pulls back the curtain—
and the world, it turns out,
is much bigger and messier
than Habakkuk ever imagined.
But it's not the answer Habakkuk wants.
He doesn't want to hear about the Chaldeans,
the ruthless empire coming for Judah.
He doesn't want to hear that God's justice
might look different from what he expected.
He doesn't want to hear that sometimes the good
have to sit in the tension
while God works out something beyond their understanding.
And so, Habakkuk argues.
He wrestles with God,
like a prophet who knows he's in the ring with the Creator,
but still wants to throw a few punches.
In the end, though,
after all the questions and complaints,
after the wrestling and the wondering,
Habakkuk decides—
or rather, chooses—to trust.
He knows the righteous will live by faith,
and so he says,
*Though the fig tree does not bud
and there are no grapes on the vines,
though the olive crop fails
and the fields produce no food,
though there are no sheep in the pen*

and no cattle in the stalls,
yet I will rejoice in the Lord,
I will be joyful in God my Savior.
It's a strange conclusion,
isn't it?
After all the complaining,
the questioning,
the wrestling—
he ends with joy.
I close the book,
smiling at the word *Habakkuk* itself,
which is fun to say,
but even more fun to think about—
because in the end,
maybe that's what faith is:
the ability to wrestle,
to complain,
and then,
to choose joy anyway.

THE DAY OF THE LORD

There is a crazy man on the corner,
waving his arms,
trying to get everyone's attention.
The day of the Lord is coming,
and it won't be the kind of day
you plan a picnic for.
This isn't a day for singing
or for family barbecues.
No, this is a day of wrath,
of judgment,
of reckoning.
It's hard to read.
Zephaniah doesn't mince words.
He speaks of a day
when the sky will darken,
when the earth will tremble,
when people will be caught off guard
by the very thing they've been ignoring:
their own failure,
their own arrogance.
But it's not just the big cities
Zephaniah's worried about.
No, even the remote places,
the small towns and villages,
they won't escape this day.

Every person who has turned away,
every heart that has lifted itself in pride—
they'll be swept up in the tide
of what's coming.
It's not a pleasant picture,
but Zephaniah doesn't leave us there.
No, he's got something else—
a tiny sliver of hope
hidden in the middle of all this doom.
For those who seek God,
for those who humble themselves,
there's refuge.
There's safety.
There's a remnant.
A group of people who will survive the storm,
and after the tempest has passed,
they will sing again.
They'll sing a song of joy,
because in the end,
God is not just a judge.
God is also a shepherd,
and this day,
as terrible as it may seem,
is the beginning of something new.
I close the book,
thinking about how quickly we forget
that judgment and mercy are often two sides
of the same coin,
and how, sometimes,
the worst things we face
are the very things that make us see
the grace we never thought we deserved.

THE REBUILDING

This one walks through the rubble,
his sandals kicking up dust
that hasn't been disturbed in years.
The temple lies in ruins,
a hollow shell that once echoed with song,
now silent, like an old song forgotten.
He doesn't sugarcoat it.
You're sitting in your paneled houses,
he says to the people,
while the house of the Lord lies in ruins.
The people look around,
awkwardly shifting on their feet,
aware that their priorities are out of whack.
They've been busy building their own comforts,
fixing their own little kingdoms,
while the work of God's house has been left behind.
Haggai's message is simple:
It's time to rebuild.
It's time to stop making excuses
about the bad economy,
about the lack of resources,
about how hard things have been.
Because, he says,
God's promise is still good.
The glory of this house
will be greater than the former glory.

The best is yet to come.
There's something surprisingly practical in all this.
Haggai doesn't waste time talking about philosophy
or about lofty ideals.
He doesn't even ask for a heart change first—
he tells them to *get to work*.
Build, he says,
and I'll be with you.
It's almost like he's saying,
Do what you can,
and watch me do the rest.
So they do.
They roll up their sleeves,
dust off their tools,
and they begin to rebuild.
And, sure enough,
the work goes on,
the temple begins to rise again,
and God's presence starts to feel a little more real.
I close the book,
thinking about how often I've sat,
waiting for a feeling to stir before I act,
when maybe I've been waiting for the wrong thing.
Sometimes the work comes first—
and the blessing follows.

THE DREAMER'S CALL

Zechariah wakes up in the middle of the night,
his heart racing,
his mind filled with visions.
He rubs his eyes,
wondering if he's still dreaming.
But no,
it's real—
the night is alive with strange,
colorful,
and downright bizarre images.
A man on a red horse.
Four horsemen with banners.
A flying scroll.
A woman in a basket,
sealed tight like a jar of pickles.
Zechariah doesn't know what to make of it,
but he knows one thing—
he's being shown something important.
God's message is clear:
Return to me,
and I will return to you.
It's not just a call for the people of Israel;
it's a promise that God is still invested,
still interested,
still active in their story.

The work isn't over,
the temple isn't finished,
and the future isn't set in stone.
But there's a twist,
a kind of cosmic rearranging.
Zechariah sees a vision of a high priest,
Joshua, standing before the angel of the Lord—
his clothes filthy,
but God, in all His grace,
takes them off and gives him new garments,
clean and shining.
It's a picture of forgiveness,
a picture of restoration,
and it's the kind of image
that makes Zechariah's head spin.
The visions keep coming—
a golden lampstand,
a flying scroll,
and then, in the middle of it all,
the promise:
I will bring my servant, the Branch.
The people are waiting for something,
someone—
a leader,
a king,
a messiah to come.
And Zechariah gets a glimpse of it.
But there's something else in these dreams,
something a little more unsettling:
the road ahead won't be easy.

There's still opposition,
there's still brokenness,
there's still a lot of work to be done.
But God will not abandon them.
I close the book,
still thinking about Zechariah's visions—
strange, puzzling,
and yet full of hope.
It's like he's trying to speak in a language
that's half dream, half reality,
a reminder that the world we see
isn't always the world that's true.
Maybe we need to look at the shadows sometimes
to see the light.

THE LAST WORD

Malachi stands on the edge of the Old Testament,
looking back at the long road they've traveled,
the centuries of prophecy,
the cycles of rebellion and repentance,
and now, after all of it,
the final word comes—
sharp, quick, like a thunderclap.
It's a reminder,
a rebuke,
and a plea all in one.
Where's the honor I deserve?
God asks,
Why have you brought me your leftovers?
The people stand there,
squirming under the weight of their neglect,
their half-hearted offerings,
their indifferent worship.
Malachi doesn't mince words.
The priests have failed.
The people have failed.
And the whole system has become a charade,
a hollow shell of what it was meant to be.
But the message isn't just a critique;
it's a wake-up call.
There's still time to turn things around.
There's still a chance for a change of heart,
a return to genuine devotion.

And then, like a sudden gust of wind,
the tone shifts.
God promises that He will send a messenger,
a messenger who will prepare the way
for something greater,
someone greater.
The day is coming,
He says,
a day of refinement,
like a refiner's fire.
This day will burn away the impurities,
clear away the rust,
and leave only what's pure.
And at the end of it all,
the last word Malachi gives
is one of hope.
The sun of righteousness will rise,
with healing in its wings.
It's not the end of the story,
but a pause,
a pregnant silence before the next chapter.
It's a quiet promise that, though the wait may be long,
the fulfillment is coming.
I close the book,
and the silence lingers.
There's a weight to these final words,
like the last note of a song that fades out,
leaving you waiting for the next movement,
knowing that the end is never really the end,
but always the beginning of something else.

Part 2

The New Testament

THE GENEALOGY

Matthew opens his book with a family tree—
not the kind you'd find at a holiday dinner,
but one with names like Abraham, David, and Joseph.
He traces the lineage,
names you've probably never heard of,
and then, right in the middle,
he drops it:
And Mary, the mother of Jesus,
who is called the Messiah.
It's not exactly the opening of a bestseller.
No dramatic entrance,
no angels singing from the heavens.
Just a genealogy—
an unassuming list of names
that somehow tie the very beginning of everything
to a carpenter's son in a small town.
Matthew doesn't waste time on fluff.
He gets straight to the point:
this is the one.
The promised King,
the fulfillment of ages of waiting.
The birth of Jesus is announced with fanfare,
but Matthew doesn't care about the fanfare.
He doesn't dwell on the star,
or the shepherds,
or the magi with their gold, frankincense, and myrrh.

He tells you who He is,
and then he begins with the work—
the healing, the teaching, the miracles.
He shows us a Messiah who isn't just a King in a palace,
but a King who walks with the broken,
who dines with sinners,
who flips tables in the temple,
who tells stories about mustard seeds
and buried treasure.
Matthew's Jesus isn't soft,
and He isn't safe.
He's a teacher with authority,
a healer with compassion,
and a King who'll die on a cross
for the very people who've rejected Him.
The Sermon on the Mount is filled with blessings,
but also with challenges—
blessings for the poor in spirit,
the meek,
the hungry,
the persecuted.
It's the upside-down Kingdom where the first are last,
and the last are first.
And then there are the parables—
the stories that turn everything on its head,
like the one about the workers in the vineyard,
who all get paid the same,
no matter how long they worked.
It's unfair,
it's baffling,
and it's grace.

Matthew brings it all to a climax,
with the cross,
and with the resurrection—
the moment when the story changes forever,
the moment when hope bursts forth
like light through the darkest night.
I close the book,
and I think about how much we love a good story—
but sometimes, we forget that a good story
is never really over.
Matthew leaves us with a command to go,
to make disciples,
to share this good news,
to carry this strange, upside-down Kingdom
into the world.
Because the story isn't done.
It's just begun.

THE IMMEDIATE

Mark doesn't waste time.
He doesn't start with a genealogy,
or a long, drawn-out prologue.
No, he just dives in—
The beginning of the good news about Jesus the Messiah, the Son of God.
That's it.
No fluff, no fanfare.
From the moment the gospel starts,
it's all action.
John the Baptist appears,
wild and loud,
proclaiming the kingdom of God is near—
and then Jesus shows up,
getting baptized like everyone else,
as if to say, *Yes, even I need this.*
Even I enter in like this.
Immediately—
that's Mark's favorite word.
It pops up over and over,
pushing the story forward with the speed of someone in a hurry.
No sooner does Jesus step out of the water than He's led into the wilderness.
He's tempted,
He's tested,
and He's back before you know it,
calling disciples and healing the sick.

There's no time to stop for a breath.
Mark's Jesus is on a mission,
moving through the towns and villages,
healing the blind,
casting out demons,
stilling storms,
and teaching with parables that make you scratch your head.
He speaks in riddles,
His actions defy the status quo,
and He always has an answer that stings just a little.
His disciples?
Well, they're a mess.
They get it wrong almost every time,
their questions are awkward,
their faith is small.
But Jesus keeps moving forward,
because the mission is urgent.
And just when you think things are getting clearer,
Mark pulls the rug out from under you.
Jesus, the Son of God,
the Messiah,
the Healer of the sick,
the Restorer of sight—
He's arrested.
He's betrayed.
He's crucified.
The whole thing takes a turn you don't see coming.
In Mark's world,
there are no long speeches,
no emotional goodbyes.
There's just a cross,

a cry of abandonment,
and a lifeless body.
The climax is quick,
almost brutal in its swiftness.
But then, like a flash of light,
He's risen.
The women run to the tomb,
find it empty,
and the angel says it:
He is not here. He has risen.
I close the book,
thinking about how Mark's Jesus never slows down.
There's always a sense of urgency,
a call to follow,
to act,
to move.
It's not a story to sit with and ponder,
but one to jump into,
feet first.
The gospel, in Mark's hands,
is a flash of light
and a call to get moving.

THE LAUGHTER OF ANGELS

Luke begins like someone carefully setting the stage,
telling us who's in charge,
what year it is,
and who's the high priest—
as if to say,
This isn't just a story. This is history.
And then he opens the curtain,
and there's the angel,
coming to Zechariah in the temple,
announcing the impossible:
Your wife, Elizabeth, will have a son.
And Zechariah, like any sane person,
doubts it.
Who wouldn't?
But the angel, undeterred,
makes Zechariah mute
as a reminder:
This is not the work of humans.
This is God's doing.
But Luke's not just about impossible births.
He's about the unexpected,
the surprising people who get caught up in God's story.
Like Mary,
a young girl from nowhere,
who hears the angel's words and responds,
Let it be to me as you have said.

No arguments.
No hesitation.
Just a quiet willingness to be swept up in the divine plan.
And then, of course, there's the birth.
Luke, with his gentle hand,
describes it all—the manger,
the shepherds in the fields,
and the angels singing—
Glory to God in the highest,
and on earth, peace to those on whom His favor rests.
It's the kind of announcement that makes you feel small,
and yet, incredibly loved,
like the whole universe just stopped to take a breath
and say, *Look. It's happening.*
But this isn't just a sweet Christmas story.
Luke's Jesus is on a mission,
gathering the outcasts and the sinners,
and telling stories about lost things—
a lost sheep,
a lost coin,
a lost son.
He's the kind of person who invites people to the table
who have no business being there,
and who changes the rules
of who's in and who's out.
He doesn't walk around with a sense of superiority.
He's the friend of tax collectors,
the healer of lepers,
the forgiver of adulterers.
And His message is clear:
The kingdom of God isn't a place for the righteous.

It's a place for the broken,
the hungry,
the poor,
and the hurting.
But even as He shows grace,
there's a fire in His words,
a call to repentance,
to turn and live differently.
The rich are warned.
The proud are humbled.
The proud are shown mercy,
and the lost are invited to a feast.
I close the book,
feeling like I've been part of something larger than myself,
a story full of twists,
turns, and unexpected characters.
Luke's gospel is like a long, comforting embrace,
full of laughter and tenderness,
but with a warning in the wings:
The kingdom is near,
and it's not just for the ones you expect.
It's for you,
and it's for me.

IN THE BEGINNING WAS THE WORD

This one doesn't start with a genealogy,
or a birth narrative,
or even a neat little introduction.
This one starts with a cosmic declaration—
In the beginning was the Word,
and the Word was with God,
and the Word was God.
As if to say,
Forget what you know.
This isn't just another story.
This is the story.
No shepherds in fields here.
No wise men with gifts.
Just the Word,
moving through the universe like a whisper,
a force,
a presence.
John doesn't make small talk—
he goes straight for the jugular,
telling you that Jesus isn't just a man,
or a prophet,
or a healer.
He's the Logos,
the divine reason that holds the whole universe together,
the light that shines in the darkness,
the life that is the light of all people.

From there, we're swept up into the details—
the signs,
the miracles,
the conversations.
Jesus turning water into wine
as if to say,
The party's just begun.
Healing a blind man and saying,
Whoever follows me will never walk in darkness.
Feeding thousands with a boy's lunch
and teaching them,
I am the Bread of Life.
But John's Jesus is different—
He's not as concerned with parables
or polite conversations.
He's confrontational.
He doesn't hide His identity.
He speaks in riddles that make your head spin,
I am the vine,
you are the branches.
I and the Father are one.
Before Abraham was, I am.
There's a boldness here that doesn't sit well with everyone.
The religious leaders don't know what to make of Him.
The crowds don't always understand.
But He keeps going,
and with every step,
the tension builds.
John's Jesus is also the one who weeps—
at Lazarus's tomb,
He cries.

Jesus wept.
It's the shortest verse in the Bible,
but it's the deepest.
Because in John,
Jesus doesn't just perform miracles.
He enters into our pain.
He stands with us in our grief.
And then comes the cross—
not as a tragic ending,
but as the climax.
Jesus doesn't just die.
He gives Himself up willingly.
No one takes it from me, He says,
but I lay it down of my own accord.
The cross is where everything is undone,
and yet, it's where everything is made whole.
The resurrection comes,
and John doesn't waste time on the empty tomb.
He focuses on the appearance—
the risen Jesus,
standing in the garden,
calling Mary by name.
And suddenly,
everything makes sense.
I close the book,
and I feel like I've been drawn into a world that's both vast and intimate,
a world where light and darkness wrestle,
where life and death are not opposites but companions,
and where the Word became flesh
and lived among us.

John's gospel is the kind that makes you want to believe,
and at the same time,
it leaves you questioning everything you thought you knew.
Because it's not just a story.
It's the story that changes everything.

THE ONGOING

There is a question—
Lord, are you at this moment going to restore the kingdom to Israel?
And Jesus, always the one who redefines things,
answers,
It's not for you to know times or seasons.
And then—Go.
Wait.
You'll receive power.
With that, He ascends—
leaving them staring at the sky,
like kids watching their balloons float away.
And instead of offering an answer,
He gives them a mission.
A Holy Spirit.
And a promise:
You will be my witnesses.
That's how Acts begins.
With a promise and a blank page.
It's a story of *the church*—
a term we throw around so much,
we forget it's a living, breathing thing,
like a plant that grows and sprawls,
sometimes wild, sometimes contained,
but always reaching for the light.
The apostles begin with a bang,
preaching,

healing,
casting out demons,
and watching the world shift around them.
Peter, the same guy who denied Jesus,
now stands in front of thousands,
boldly declaring,
Repent and be baptized,
every one of you,
in the name of Jesus Christ.
Three thousand people are baptized in a single day.
It's like a flood,
and the church is born,
like a newborn gasping for air,
filling the room,
filling the streets.
But it's not all miracles and crowds.
The church is also full of tension,
divisions,
and disagreements.
Who gets to eat with whom?
Who's in, and who's out?
And then there's the whole issue of Gentiles.
What do we do with them?
And along comes Saul.
No, scratch that—
Paul.
The guy who was hunting Christians,
and now—
now he's one of them.
And his story is the one that really gets you.
Because Paul is everywhere.

He's on ships,
in prisons,
before kings.
And no matter what happens,
he keeps moving,
keeps preaching,
keeps writing letters
that will eventually become the very foundation of our faith.
The church keeps growing,
but it's not easy.
They face opposition from all sides—
from the religious,
from the political,
from their own doubts.
But they don't quit.
They keep going.
Acts isn't a nice, neat little story with a bow on top.
It's a saga,
an unfolding adventure of broken people,
empowered by the Holy Spirit,
pushing forward into the unknown.
I close the book,
and I realize—
the story hasn't ended.
We're still in it.
Still trying to live out the mission.
Still answering the call to be witnesses,
to be the church.
Still asking:

What does it mean to follow Jesus in a world that doesn't always understand?

And somewhere,
in the middle of the struggle,
the church keeps moving forward.
Not because of us,
but because of the Spirit
who has never stopped working,
never stopped leading,
never stopped breathing life
into what's still unfolding.

THE LETTER

Paul begins with a greeting,
like a letter you might never send,
but still, it matters.
He writes to the Romans,
but really, he writes to all of us—
to the ones sitting in church pews
and to the ones who've never stepped foot in a church,
to the wise and to the foolish,
to those who think they've got it all together,
and to those who feel like they've got nothing.
He tells them what they already know—
we're all in trouble.
Sin is like a weight
that drags us to the bottom of the sea,
and the law?
It just shows us how deep we are in it.
It's a mirror that reflects everything wrong,
but offers no way out.
Paul doesn't sugarcoat it—
we've all fallen short.
Not one of us is righteous.
It's a hard pill to swallow,
but it's the truth,
and without it, we'd never understand grace.
But then—
the twist,

the sudden breath of air,
the good news that changes everything—
but now, apart from the law, the righteousness of God has been made known.
Through Jesus.
Through His death.
Through His resurrection.
It's not about being good enough.
It's about believing.
Trusting.
Placing our hearts in the hands of the One who said,
It is finished.
The rest of the letter is a journey—
through faith and works,
grace and struggle,
life and death.
Paul writes like someone who's just figured out the meaning of the universe
and is trying to tell you in one breath.
He talks about being justified by faith,
about peace with God,
about the Holy Spirit coming into our lives
like a visitor who refuses to leave.
He says,
For the wages of sin is death,
but the gift of God is eternal life in Christ Jesus our Lord.
Then, he lays it out—
how we should live in response to this gift,
not as if we're earning it,
but as if it's already ours.
He paints a picture of a new kind of life,
one where love is genuine,

where enemies are loved,
where peace is pursued.
And all the while, he insists—
this is not a life we can pull off on our own.
This is the power of the Holy Spirit,
working in us.
Romans is a letter that will make you uncomfortable.
It will make you wrestle with grace,
with justice,
with mercy.
It'll make you face the hard truths of who you are
while showing you who you could be.
It's a mirror that doesn't just reflect.
It transforms.
I close the book,
and I feel like I've just read the instructions for a life
that I'm not sure I'm ready for,
but one I can't stop thinking about.
The letter is an invitation,
and I know I've been invited.
It's not about me making the first move.
It's about Jesus making the first move,
and now—
I get to respond.

THE LETTER TO THE DIVIDED

Paul opens with a kind of warmth
that feels like a handshake,
a pat on the back—
I thank my God always for you,
because of the grace of God
that has been given you in Christ Jesus.
But it doesn't take long
before he starts poking at the seams.
You can almost hear him muttering,
Guys, I've got to address some things.
The Corinthians are a mess.
Oh, they're gifted, alright—
they speak in tongues,
they prophesy,
they perform miracles,
but they're also divided,
proud,
arguing over who baptized whom,
who's the better preacher,
who has the best spiritual gift.
It's like a group of people
who've received invitations to the same wedding,
but they're too busy fighting over who gets to sit at the head table.
Paul writes,
reminding them that the church isn't a popularity contest—
it's not about the strongest preacher,

the most eloquent speaker,
or the flashiest miracle worker.
Christ crucified is the only thing that matters.
For the foolishness of God is wiser than human wisdom,
and the weakness of God is stronger than human strength.
That's the starting point,
and that's where everything has to land.
But Paul doesn't stop there.
He goes deep—
and by deep, I mean deep,
like swimming in a sea of difficult truths.
He talks about the foolishness of human wisdom,
how the cross doesn't make sense
to those who think they have it all figured out.
He talks about how they're spiritual infants,
drinking milk when they should be eating solid food.
There's division in the church,
and Paul's not here to patch things up with duct tape.
He calls it like it is—
You're still worldly.
This church, he says,
has become like a dysfunctional family,
bickering over trivial things,
while forgetting the core of the gospel.
Is Christ divided?
Were you baptized in the name of Paul?
The letter gets messy—
like a long argument that you didn't know how to stop,
but it keeps pushing,
because the Corinthians need to hear it.
Paul doesn't hold back.

He talks about lawsuits between believers,
sexual immorality,
and how the body isn't just a vessel to be used however we please.
It's a temple.
A dwelling place for the Holy Spirit.
Yet, in the midst of all the correction,
Paul never forgets the gospel of grace.
It's all about Jesus—
His death and resurrection.
The church exists not for personal gain,
not to make us feel good about ourselves,
but to glorify God
and to live as if we've been crucified with Christ.
And that means laying down everything
that doesn't honor Him.
In the final chapters,
Paul talks about love—
the most excellent way.
The very thing the Corinthians were missing,
in their wisdom,
in their gifts,
in their endless debates—
Love.
Not as a nice idea,
but as the power that holds everything together.
If I speak in the tongues of men or of angels,
but do not have love,
I am only a resounding gong or a clanging cymbal.
I close the book,
and I'm left with the sound of cymbals ringing in my ears,
and the sharp sting of conviction.

Paul has given us more than instructions;
he's given us a glimpse of the church
that should be,
could be.
And yet, I know—
the story isn't over,
the letter isn't finished.
It's a mirror,
and it's not just for the Corinthians.
It's for all of us.

THE LETTER OF TEARS

Paul starts with his defense—
a bit like a man standing in front of a courtroom,
sweat on his brow,
facing accusations from a people who should have known better.
His heart is heavy,
but he presses on,
I don't regret sending that first letter,
even though it made you weep.
He's talking about the "letter of sorrow,"
the one that stung like a bee and made the Corinthians squirm.
But sometimes,
Paul says,
tears are necessary.
Because it's through pain that we find repentance,
and through repentance, we find life.
He calls himself a *servant*—
not just a servant,
but a servant *of the new covenant*,
which isn't about the letter of the law
but about the Spirit.
And he contrasts the old and the new,
like comparing a black-and-white movie
with a burst of color.
The glory of the old covenant—
the law, the rules, the punishment—
was good for its time,
but the new covenant?

It's life-changing.
It's the Spirit of the living God
writing His law on hearts,
not stone tablets.
But let's be real—
Paul's not just talking about how awesome the new covenant is.
He's dealing with some real mess.
The Corinthians are still the Corinthians—
divided, opinionated,
and quick to turn their backs.
They've got enemies,
Paul's enemies,
and the accusations against him are mounting.
He's weak.
He's unreliable.
He's just a man, like any other.
But Paul leans in,
telling them that the weakness they see in him
is actually where God's strength is displayed.
It's like the cracked pottery,
broken but holding the treasure inside.
We have this treasure in jars of clay,
he writes,
to show that this all-surpassing power is from God and not from us.
Paul's ministry isn't one of glory and ease.
It's one of hardship,
persecution,
and the kind of suffering that makes you question your sanity.
But Paul's okay with that.
In fact,
he's proud of it.

Because his life—
his very ministry—
points to something greater than himself.
It points to Christ.
For Christ's sake, we are weak,
but in Him, we are strong.
As he writes,
you can feel the weight of the letter
pressing down on him.
He's not writing for applause or approval.
He's writing to keep the Corinthians from drifting off course,
to remind them of the gospel that has already been preached.
God was reconciling the world to Himself in Christ,
not counting people's sins against them.
But Paul's also a pastor,
and you get the sense that he's sitting in a room,
nervously glancing at the door,
wondering if his words will reach the hearts of the ones he's desperately trying to save.
The church is fragile.
But grace,
grace is stronger than their divisions.
It's stronger than their mistakes.
As the letter winds down,
Paul moves from defense to encouragement—
You are not just the body of Christ.
You are the temple of the living God.
There's an urgency in his voice—
a plea that they live up to their calling,
that they become who they were always meant to be.
I close the book,

and it's almost like I can feel the sweat of the ink on the page.
Paul has bared his soul,
exposing his vulnerability,
his weakness,
and the cost of living out the gospel.
It's a hard letter,
but a necessary one.
For the Corinthians,
for us,
for all who follow after Christ.
And somewhere in between the lines,
I hear Paul's voice,
We are not made for easy lives.
We are made for the glory of God—
weak,
fragile,
but made strong in Christ.

THE LETTER THAT BURNS

Paul opens with a sharp word,
no pleasantries, no small talk—
I am astonished
he writes,
as if he just walked into a room
to find a fine meal turned to ashes.
The Galatians,
whom he has labored over,
are already flirting with disaster.
Who has bewitched you?
he demands,
Before your very eyes Jesus Christ was clearly portrayed as crucified.
He's angry,
and it's the kind of anger
that carries the weight of love.
The Galatians are being swayed by new teachings,
by people who want to put them back under the law,
as if grace isn't enough,
as if Jesus' sacrifice wasn't the end of the story.
Paul says no,
no,
there is no other gospel.
If someone is preaching a gospel other than the one we preached to you,
let them be under God's curse.
He's harsh,
but it's the fire of a parent scolding a child
for forgetting who they are.

Because, for Paul, this isn't just about doctrine.
It's about identity.
The Galatians are forgetting their freedom.
They're slipping back into chains
when they've already been set free.
The whole letter feels like an urgent plea,
a reminder that the gospel is not about
doing all the right things,
following all the right rules,
jumping through all the hoops.
It's about Christ,
who loved us and gave Himself for us.
It's about grace,
unearned,
unmerited,
unfathomable.
For freedom, Christ has set us free.
Paul uses the law like a mirror—
not to say, *You've failed*,
but to say, *This is what you needed*
until Christ came.
The law was a tutor,
a guide,
but it never had the power to save.
Now that Christ has come,
the law has no claim on you anymore.
It's like telling a child,
You don't need the training wheels anymore.
But just because they've been set free
doesn't mean the Galatians should live like wild children,
eating candy and running through traffic.

No,
freedom in Christ looks like love,
and love looks like serving one another.
Paul talks about the *fruit of the Spirit*,
which is no longer about checking boxes—
but about *love, joy, peace, forbearance, kindness, goodness, faithfulness, gentleness, and self-control.*
You'll know someone is free
when their life looks like that.
Paul's voice softens at times—
I am in the pains of childbirth
until Christ is formed in you.
He's a mother in labor,
he's a father with a heavy heart,
he's a preacher trying to get through to a church
that's forgetting the basics.
He ends the letter by reminding them
of the new creation.
Neither circumcision nor uncircumcision means anything;
what counts is the new creation.
It's like a tattoo,
but not one on the skin—
a mark on the heart,
a permanent change.
The gospel is not about reforming you;
it's about transforming you.
The only thing that counts is faith expressing itself through love.
I close the book,
and it feels like something's been stirred,
something I didn't even know was asleep.
Paul has spoken to us like a coach,

like a parent,
like someone who sees the best in us
and refuses to let us settle for anything less.
The gospel isn't just a nice story,
it's a fire,
and it burns away everything that doesn't matter,
leaving only Christ and His love.
And now, the letter is done.
But I can still hear the echoes,
still feel the heat on my skin.
Grace,
grace,
grace.
It's not just a word—
it's the whole game.

THE LETTER TO THE ONES WHO ARE ALREADY SEATED

Paul begins with a kind of spiritual thunder,
like the beginning of a symphony,
Blessed be the God and Father of our Lord Jesus Christ,
and in the space of one breath,
he spills out a whole universe of blessing.
You can almost hear the grandiosity of it,
a world made,
a people chosen,
a destiny mapped out.
He chose us in Him before the foundation of the world,
and suddenly,
we're all caught up in the story
of things much bigger than us.
There's something almost too vast to grasp here—
Paul isn't talking about just what's happening now,
but about the *before*
and the *after*.
Before the world was even a thought,
God had us in mind.
That's heady stuff.
And now,
in this very moment,
we sit *in the heavenly realms* with Christ.
We're not waiting to get there,
we're already there,
seated with Him.

It's like Paul just pulls us into the eternal and says,
This is your present reality.
Paul praises God for grace—
not the "I'll let you off the hook" kind of grace,
but the kind that makes us who we are,
the kind that doesn't just forgive,
but *transforms.*
You can almost see him,
writing with such passion,
he has to pause and catch his breath.
In Him,
we have redemption through His blood,
and we were *predestined to be adopted*
into God's family.
This is not just a nice idea,
it's our inheritance.
There's a rhythm to this letter,
almost like a dance.
It moves from the cosmos to the personal,
from *we* to *you.*
And Paul reminds us that the church is this grand mystery—
the plan of the ages now revealed:
Christ in you, the hope of glory.
It's a bit absurd,
if you stop to think about it—
us, with Christ in us?
It's like trying to fit the ocean into a teacup.
But Paul doesn't let up.
He moves from the *glory of salvation*
to the *calling of the church.*

We are one body,
united,
broken into pieces,
yet somehow whole.
He tells us to *walk worthy*—
to live in such a way that our lives reflect what's already true of us in Christ.
And the way we walk
is in humility,
gentleness,
and patience—
qualities we often like to *talk* about,
but not always live out.
There's a beautiful mess here—
because the church is a group of people,
and people are . . . complicated.
But Paul isn't naive.
He doesn't deny the difficulty of unity,
he just insists on it.
He *commands* us to be one,
to remember that we are all parts of one body,
and that if one part hurts,
we all hurt.
It's not *if* we are united,
it's *how*.
And then there's the classic image:
Put on the full armor of God.
It's the kind of metaphor you'd expect from a warrior-poet—
but Paul's not just playing dress-up here.
This armor is for real battles,
for wrestling against the powers and principalities,

and yes,
we will wrestle.
But we wrestle with truth,
righteousness,
peace,
faith,
and salvation—
these are our weapons.
Then, at the end, Paul gives us this prayer—
a prayer for strength,
for power,
but not in the sense we usually think.
Not for success,
not for wealth,
but for the *power to grasp how wide and long and high and deep is the love of Christ.*
It's a prayer for *more of Him*
and for us to be filled with all the fullness of God.
And you wonder,
if that's all we had,
would it be enough?
I close the letter,
and I sit for a second.
Paul hasn't just written to the Ephesians—
he's written to all of us.
He's written a love letter to the church,
to the ones who have already been seated with Christ,
but are still figuring out how to walk on earth.
It's like a cosmic reminder:
You are part of something bigger than yourself.
And as I put the letter down,

I find myself wondering—
if I truly *believed* this,
what would change?
How would I walk differently?
What armor would I wear tomorrow?
I close my eyes,
and I think about the love,
so wide and long and high and deep,
that it cannot be measured.
It's the love we are already swimming in.
And that,
my friend,
is enough.

THE LETTER FROM THE JAILHOUSE

Paul writes from a place of chains,
but you wouldn't know it
by the joy in his words.
He begins with a greeting,
but it's not just any greeting—
Grace and peace
like a gift that falls from heaven
and lands in your lap.
From jail,
he sends out these soft words,
as if nothing could steal his joy—
not the guards,
not the bars,
not the cold floor beneath him.
He tells them how much he longs for them—
I thank my God every time I remember you.
It's the kind of thankfulness
that makes the heart warm
even when the body is cold.
And then, he speaks of something more than friendship,
something deeper than affection—
a partnership in the gospel.
They're in this together,
all of them,
working side by side in the greatest mission of all.
And he's confident.

*He who began a good work in you
will carry it on to completion
until the day of Christ Jesus.*
There's a sweet irony here—
Paul, sitting in chains,
is the one telling them to rejoice.
He's the one urging them to *stand firm*
in the Lord,
to *rejoice always*,
to let their *gentleness be evident to all*.
But isn't it just like Paul to speak of joy
from a prison cell,
to call for peace
from a place of strife?
His joy doesn't depend on circumstances.
It's rooted in something deeper—
a love that doesn't leave you,
no matter the walls that surround you.
He gives them a little pep talk:
Do nothing out of selfish ambition or vain conceit.
But what he really means is,
Think of the other person first.
It's the heart of the gospel,
wrapped up in the smallest, simplest, most difficult thing—
humility.
In humility, value others above yourselves.
Not as a strategy,
but as a way of life.
Then, he tells them about Christ,
who did not consider His divinity
something to be used for His own advantage,
but emptied Himself.

He took the lowest place,
became obedient to death,
even death on a cross.
And because of that,
God has exalted Him,
given Him the name above every name.
It's the great reversal,
the upside-down kingdom,
where humility leads to glory.
Paul, in his chains, knows the secret—
I can do all this through Him who gives me strength.
He's learned to be content,
whether he has much or little,
whether his body is well or sick,
whether his future is certain or unknown.
And now, he shares that secret with them:
it's not the circumstances that shape you,
but Christ.
The joy, the strength, the peace—
it all comes from Him.
Then, the letter turns personal.
Paul thanks them for the gift they sent him,
but even in his thanks,
there's an unmistakable humility.
He says, *Not that I am looking for a gift,*
but I am looking for what may be credited to your account.
He's the one in need,
and yet, he sees their gift as part of their own spiritual growth,
as a way of participating in the bigger work of God.
It's like he's always looking for the lesson,
the holy ripple effect

in every little thing.
And then, as he wraps up,
he gives them one more word of encouragement:
Rejoice in the Lord always.
Not when things are going well,
but always.
And just in case they didn't get it,
he says it again:
Rejoice!
It's as if,
no matter where you are—
in chains or in freedom,
in sickness or in health—
the gospel calls you to joy.
I close the letter,
and I can't help but smile.
Paul's joy is contagious,
even from a distance.
He shows us that joy isn't about what we have,
but about what we know—
that God is with us,
that He is at work in us,
that He is our strength,
our peace,
our joy.
And that's the kind of joy
that doesn't depend on the situation,
the kind of joy that you can carry with you
wherever you go—
even in chains.

LETTER TO THE DISCONNECTED

Paul writes as if to a church
that has started to lose its way,
not in a grand, tragic way,
but in the quiet, creeping manner
of slowly forgetting what matters.
He starts with gratitude,
a thankful note that seems to hold the world together.
We always thank God, the Father of our Lord Jesus Christ,
and for a moment, you wonder if the letter is a lullaby—
a reminder that no matter how scattered we feel,
there is always something to give thanks for.
But then the tone shifts,
like the sound of a door creaking open.
Paul starts to tell them what they need—
the *fullness* of Christ.
In Him, all things were created,
things in heaven and on earth,
visible and invisible.
It's the kind of language that could make anyone's head spin—
but Paul isn't trying to get them to think,
he's trying to get them to *see*
the mystery of it all.
Everything,
he says,
everything points back to Christ.
He is the center,
the axis around which all things turn.

Then comes the mystery of reconciliation—
Christ, through the cross,
reconciling the world to God.
Once you were alienated from God—
and here, Paul's words feel like a quiet tug at the heart.
Alienated—
separated—
cut off—
but through Christ,
you are now reconciled.
And it's not just a forgiveness of sins,
it's a full-blown restoration,
like a door that was closed for years
suddenly swinging wide open,
and you walk through it to find everything
you had forgotten.
Paul knows the dangers of drifting—
there's always someone ready to tell them the next big thing,
the latest philosophy,
the newest trend.
See to it that no one takes you captive through hollow and deceptive philosophy,
he warns.
It's almost as if he's telling them,
Stop searching for the new,
when the answer is already here.
Christ,
the fullness of God,
is everything.
And once you have Him,
you don't need to look for anything else.

It's a letter that might make you uncomfortable—
Paul doesn't sugarcoat it.
He talks about death,
but not in a morbid way,
just the fact that we've died with Christ.
Since then, you have been raised with Christ,
he says,
and suddenly, the language feels less about the future
and more about the now—
like a secret you've always known but never said aloud:
You've already been raised.
And then, the invitation comes,
quietly and without fanfare.
Set your hearts on things above,
where Christ is seated at the right hand of God.
It's the kind of instruction that could be easy to dismiss,
but in the context of everything Paul has said,
it feels like a command to take your life back,
to remember where your true home is.
It's not about getting away from the world,
it's about remembering what is truly real—
that Christ is above it all,
and we,
we are seated with Him.
Then, Paul reminds them to live in light of this reality.
Put to death, therefore, whatever belongs to your earthly nature.
It's not a list of things to *do*,
but a gentle urging to *become*
who you already are in Christ.
Clothe yourselves with compassion, kindness, humility, gentleness and patience.

The way he says it makes it sound so simple,
like if you just *put it on*
the way you put on a jacket,
you'll be warm.
And then comes the heart of it—
the beautiful, messy part.
Forgive as the Lord forgave you.
He doesn't ask for perfect forgiveness,
just the kind that remembers how much we've been forgiven.
And above all,
Paul says,
Put on love.
It's the perfect bond of unity,
like a cloak you wrap around yourself
and everyone around you.
And as he closes,
he leaves them with this—
Let the peace of Christ rule in your hearts.
It's not an absence of trouble,
but a kind of peace that settles deep,
like a stone dropped in a still pond,
sending ripples that never stop.
I close the letter,
but it doesn't quite leave me.
It's as if the words hang in the air,
echoing back at you.
The peace of Christ,
the fullness of Christ,
the life we've already been raised to—
all of it is here.

And we're invited to step into it,
every day,
until it becomes the air we breathe.

THE LETTER OF JOY FROM THE OTHER SIDE

Paul begins, as always,
with a word of thanks,
but here, it feels more like a love letter.
We always thank God for all of you,
he writes,
and you can almost hear the warmth in his voice,
the kind of thanks that doesn't just brush past you
but stops to rest for a while.
He remembers them—
their work,
their labor,
their love.
You welcomed the message in the midst of severe suffering
with the joy given by the Holy Spirit.
And in those words,
there's something both humbling and encouraging—
that even in suffering,
joy is possible.
It's not the kind of joy that makes you smile at the right time,
but the kind that bubbles up from a place deeper than reason,
deeper than circumstance.
Paul talks about how their example has spread—
not just in the region,
but everywhere.

It's the quiet revolution of love,
no headlines,
no fanfare,
just the power of changed lives that others can't ignore.
And so he writes,
and you can feel the admiration in every line,
the awe that this little church,
this small group of believers,
has done so much.
But here's the funny thing—
Paul doesn't want to leave them there,
standing in the glow of their success.
Instead, he reminds them:
You turned to God from idols
to serve the living and true God.
It's a little bit of a *remember where you came from* moment,
but in the gentlest way possible—
as if to say,
You're not just here because you're good people,
but because something radical has happened.
They've turned from the old ways,
the things that used to hold them,
and embraced the God who holds all things together.
There's a beautiful tension in this letter—
Paul speaks of joy,
but it's a joy that doesn't ignore the real world,
the world of affliction,
the world of persecution,
the world of loss.
He doesn't sugarcoat anything,
but he also refuses to let their joy be stolen.

For we know, brothers and sisters loved by God,
that He has chosen you.
It's like he's reaching through the distance,
grabbing hold of their hearts,
reminding them of their worth.
And there's this small moment,
just a few verses in,
that feels like a peek behind the curtain:
You know how we lived among you for your sake.
It's the kind of line you almost miss,
but when you stop and think about it,
you realize—
Paul isn't just giving instructions or theology here.
He's sharing his life.
He's not asking them to do anything he hasn't done,
hasn't lived out in front of them,
and that's the power of this letter.
It's not just teaching,
it's witness.
It's Paul's life,
his joy,
his suffering,
his love for them,
all wrapped up together.
Then, Paul can't help but gush a bit more—
How you turned to God,
and how you wait for His Son from heaven.
And in those words,
there's an invitation—
a reminder that the waiting is not passive.
It's active,
it's alive.

They are *waiting* in a way that transforms the present,
serving the living and true God
while looking forward to what's coming.
I close the letter,
but Paul can't help but keep saying it from the closed book—
You are beloved,
You are chosen,
You are living proof of the gospel.
And every time he says it,
it's like he's giving them a mirror
so they can see the truth about themselves.
He reminds them of something important—
they are not in this alone.
The kingdom is not just a distant dream;
it's a present reality.
And in this shared life,
Paul speaks not just to them but to all of us—
Therefore, encourage one another
and build each other up.
It's the letter that says,
Yes, the world is hard,
but look at what you've done,
look at what you're part of,
look at what's coming.
And in that joy,
Paul ends his letter,
but his words don't quite leave you—
Rejoice always,
pray continually,
give thanks in all circumstances.

The simplicity of it stuns you,
because it doesn't ask you to do anything extraordinary,
it just asks you to live with what you already have—
a God who is with you,
a community that is for you,
a purpose that is bigger than you.
And somehow,
just like that,
you find yourself *waiting*
with a little more joy,
and a lot more hope.

THE LETTER OF STEADYING HANDS

Paul writes again,
and though the ink is different,
the heart is the same.
We ought always to thank God for you,
he begins,
as if the very act of thanking
is a holy necessity.
There's something about gratitude here—
the kind that feels earned,
earned not by circumstance but by the *way* they've lived,
with steadfast faith and love for one another,
even as the world presses in.
You can hear the warmth in Paul's words,
the way he holds them close,
like a parent checking in on a child after a storm.
Your faith is growing more and more,
he says,
and the love all of you have for one another is increasing.
The letter feels like a pat on the back,
an encouragement to keep on,
keep going,
keep growing—
because it's working.
You're doing it.
But then, as always, there's a shift—
Paul's not just here for a pep talk.

He knows their suffering.
They are enduring hardships,
for you will be counted worthy of the kingdom of God,
he writes,
and you can almost hear him whisper the words
in your own ears.
It's as if Paul knows
that suffering can either crush or shape us—
and he's convinced it's shaping them.
God is just:
Paul's words linger like a promise,
a reminder that nothing done in love,
nothing done in faith,
will go unnoticed.
God sees.
God knows.
And in that knowing,
he will bring justice.
It's not a cold, distant justice,
but one that flows from the heart of love,
the same love that holds them together,
and that will hold the world together too.
But then Paul dips into the bigger picture—
This will happen when the Lord Jesus is revealed from heaven.
It's one of those lines that sounds nice on the surface—
but deep down, you know
it carries more weight than you can carry alone.
The Lord will be revealed.
The sentence sits there,
like a truth so large
that it forces you to lean into it,

and it seems to tell you
This is what matters.
He speaks of glory—
glory, not just for Jesus,
but for those who have remained faithful.
We will be glorified in His holy people.
It's the kind of sentence you read and think,
How could I possibly be part of this?
But Paul assures them—
and you too—
that God is the one who makes this happen,
God is the one who holds the glory.
And in that glory,
we are made worthy.
Then, Paul asks something—
With this in mind, we constantly pray for you.
It's not a suggestion.
It's an invitation to live in light of the larger story,
to continue in the work that has already begun.
May our God make you worthy of His calling,
Paul prays.
And it's not a prayer of passive hope,
but one that sets their feet in a direction—
one that doesn't ask for an easy road,
but the road of faith,
the road of love.
He finishes with something profound:
The Lord is faithful,
and He will strengthen you
and protect you from the evil one.
It's not a promise of avoiding trouble,

but of having strength through it,
having peace in the middle of it.
The road ahead isn't going to be smooth,
but they won't walk it alone,
and neither will you.
Finally, Paul reminds them—
and you, and me—
that we have been called into a community of prayer,
of support,
of encouragement.
May the Lord direct your hearts into God's love
and Christ's perseverance.
Because in the end,
the strength isn't in the struggle,
but in the love that holds us,
the perseverance that carries us.
I close this letter.

PASTORAL EPISTLE WITH A CUP OF COFFEE

Paul, writing to Timothy,
but also, I think,
to anyone who has ever stared
at a congregation
like a substitute teacher
walking into a classroom
where the students
already know
the principal is out for the day.
He begins, as usual,
with grace and mercy and peace,
but you can almost hear him sigh,
because Timothy is young,
and young men with old wisdom
often find themselves
explaining the same things
again and again
to people twice their age
who still prefer
their own echo to a sermon.
Stay there in Ephesus,
Paul tells him,
which sounds less like
an assignment
and more like
a sentencing.

There are myths to untangle,
genealogies running longer
than an uncle's holiday toast,
and a few loud men
who have found a way
to weaponize the law
like a shepherd
trying to herd sheep
with a slingshot.
Paul tells Timothy
to aim for love—
a pure heart,
a good conscience,
and a sincere faith.
Three things easier to list
than to live,
especially when people
prefer an argument
to an altar.
And then Paul drifts,
as Paul does,
into autobiography.
He remembers
how he was once the worst,
the absolute worst,
a blasphemer,
a persecutor,
a violent man,
the kind of guest
you wouldn't want
at a potluck.

But mercy, he says,
mercy picked him up,
mercy made him into something
other than an old Pharisee
yelling at clouds.
Mercy made him new.
Then, in case Timothy
is wondering
why this letter
is getting a bit personal,
Paul tells him:
This is the point.
This is why you stay
in Ephesus,
even when the arguments
recycle like bad jokes.
Because Christ came for sinners,
not for the already polished,
not for the perfectly behaved,
but for the ones
who need mercy
like they need oxygen.
And then, as if
to keep Timothy
from losing his mind,
Paul tells him
to pray for everyone.
Yes, everyone.
Even the emperor,
even the difficult ones,
even the ones

who make ministry
feel like an uphill walk
in wet sandals.
There are instructions
about elders,
about deacons,
about how to live
in a world
that keeps changing
while pretending it hasn't.
Paul tells him
to watch his doctrine,
to keep his life steady,
to not neglect his gift,
which sounds lovely
until you remember
Timothy's gift
is leading these people,
and some days
that probably feels
like a bad birthday present
he can't return.
Paul closes
with practical advice:
Avoid foolish arguments.
Take care of the widows.
Keep your life simple.
Don't get tangled in money.
Be content.
Oh, and drink a little wine
for your stomach—

which is perhaps
the most relatable moment
in all of Paul's letters.
Finally, he reminds Timothy
that he is guarding something,
something real,
something alive.
Don't let anyone
talk you out of it,
he says.
Don't let the noise
make you forget
why you're here.
And so,
with a sigh,
Timothy probably
folds the letter, but I close it,
he drinks his wine,
and decides
to keep showing up
to Ephesus
one more Sunday.

FINAL INSTRUCTIONS BEFORE WINTER

Paul writes like a man
who knows the ink
is running out.
Timothy, fan the flame,
carry the gospel,
don't get tangled
in small debates
or soldier's nets.
He lists names—
some who stayed,
some who ran,
some who hurt him.
Ministry is a ledger
with more losses than wins.
He asks for a coat,
his parchments,
a few last comforts
before winter sets in.
Then, like a father
handing down
his last piece of advice,
he says—
fight the good fight,
finish the race,
keep the faith.

And just like that,
Paul is ready to go,
and Timothy
is left holding the letter,
wondering if next Sunday
will be any easier.
But what do I do but close this letter and think.

HOW TO PASTOR AN ISLAND

Paul writes to Titus,
who is stranded—not by shipwreck,
but by assignment—
on Crete, where the people
have the reputation of a bar fight
and the patience of a toddler
given a riddle.
Set things in order, Paul says,
as if the church were a room
where someone overturned the chairs
and let the wind scatter the papers.
Find good elders,
the kind who love their families
more than arguments,
who can hold their temper
and their tongue
at the same time.
Tell them grace appeared,
Paul says, as if it wandered
onto the island like a stray dog
and decided to stay.
Tell them to live like it matters,
to stop biting each other
like stray dogs themselves.
And before the ink dries,
Paul slips in a list of names,

final greetings,
instructions to visit,
and one last reminder—
do good, be good,
and don't get tangled in nonsense.
I close this letter.
And I sit with it,
wondering if pastoring
is always like this—
setting chairs upright,
chasing off stray arguments,
and hoping grace
sticks around.

PAUL, THE HOLY GUILT-TRIPPER

Paul writes to Philemon
with all the subtlety
of a grandmother
reminding you
who paid for dinner.
He starts with grace and peace,
as always,
but soon enough,
he's clearing his throat—
Now, I *could* command you,
he says,
I *could* pull rank,
but I'd rather appeal to you
as an old man,
as a prisoner,
as someone who is very,
very tired.
It's about Onesimus,
who, funny story,
used to be useless,
but now is useful—
you see what I did there?
Anyway, he's your runaway slave,
but also now your brother in Christ,
so I figured,
why not send him back

not as property,
but as family?
Oh, and if he owes you anything,
just charge it to me.
I won't mention
that you owe me
your very life.
(No pressure.)
And just when Philemon
might have had a retort ready,
Paul casually adds,
Oh, and prepare a guest room.
I'm hoping to visit soon.
It's a masterpiece, really—
a letter so dripping
with holy persuasion
that Philemon would have
to be a monster
to say no.
I close this letter,
half wondering
if Paul ever lost an argument
in his life.

A LETTER WITHOUT A NAME

The author steps onto the stage,
but the spotlight never catches their face.
No *Paul, an apostle—*
no *James, a servant—*
just words, rolling out
like thunder over Sinai.
Long ago, God spoke
through prophets, dreams,
burning bushes and whirlwinds—
but now,
now He speaks through a Son,
who sat down at the right hand
of Majesty,
which is Bible-speak for
He's in charge now.
The letter moves like a sermon
given by a preacher
who isn't afraid to look you
in the eye.
Jesus is greater—
greater than angels,
greater than Moses,
greater than priests
who grow old and die.
His sacrifice was one-and-done,
no need for daily offerings

or blood on the altar rug.
The unknown author preaches
like they've seen
too many wander off,
too many let go.
Hold fast, they say.
Don't drift, they warn.
By the end,
you're gripping the pew,
checking your grip on faith itself.
No signature at the bottom,
no *Sincerely, So-and-So,*
just the weight of history
resting in your hands.
I close this letter,
still wondering
who held the pen—
and if, maybe,
that's exactly the point.

JAMES DOESN'T MESS AROUND

No long greetings,
no warm introductions—
just James, servant of God,
hitting the ground running
like a man with no patience
for small talk.
Consider it joy when life punches you.
Ask for wisdom, but actually believe.
Stop playing favorites in church—
the rich man in gold?
Let him sit in the back.
The poor man in rags?
Give him the front row.
Faith without works is dead,
he says,
as if kicking a lifeless thing
for emphasis.
You say you believe?
Good for you.
So do demons,
and they shudder.
James has no time
for pretty words
that don't build houses,
feed stomachs,
or check in on widows.

The tongue, he says,
is a tiny flame
that can burn down
a whole forest,
which makes me want
to sit in silence
for the rest of the day.
By the end, he's still firing off
commands like a prophet
late for another appointment—
Be patient.
Don't swear oaths.
Confess your sins.
Pray for one another.
Pull back the wanderers.
And just like that,
the letter ends—
no *grace and peace*,
no soft farewell—
just the feeling
that James would be
a terrifying man
to have at your Bible study.
I close this letter,
checking my words carefully
before I speak again.

PETER WRITES TO THE SCATTERED

Peter, the rock,
the one who sank,
the one who swore,
the one who ran—
now writing letters
like a man who finally
figured things out.
To the exiles, he says,
which feels about right.
Christians, scattered
like seeds on hard soil,
trying to grow roots
in foreign lands.
Don't be surprised
when suffering knocks.
You're aliens here,
so don't expect
a housewarming gift.
Be holy, he says,
as if it were easy,
as if I didn't just
lose my temper
before opening this book.
Put away malice,
deceit, envy—
which, again, sounds nice,
but have you met people?

Still, Peter keeps going,
calling us a chosen people,
a royal priesthood,
which feels generous,
considering I just
burnt my toast this morning.
Then he turns
to submission,
to suffering,
to fiery trials—
it's all refining,
he says,
all making you
into something stronger.
By the end,
he sounds like a pastor
who has learned
to stop running.
I close this letter,
wondering if faith
is mostly about
learning to stand
where you used to sink.

PETER'S LAST WORDS

Peter writes again,
but this time,
you can feel the weight—
like an old man
settling into a chair,
knowing his time is short.
I won't be here much longer,
he says,
so let me remind you—
as if we could forget
the way he walked on water,
then sank,
the way he swore he'd never leave,
then ran.
Still, he speaks,
steady now,
warning of false teachers
with their big words
and empty stomachs,
promising freedom
while wearing their own chains.
And about the second coming—
don't get impatient.
A thousand years?
That's just a day to God.

He's not slow,
just patient,
waiting for more strays
to come home.
But don't get lazy, either.
The world will burn,
the elements will melt,
so maybe
spend less time
polishing what won't last
and more time
on holiness.
Then, one last reminder—
stick with Paul,
even if he's hard to understand.
Which is fair,
since Paul sometimes writes
like he's running late
for another city.
Peter ends with grace.
Of course he does.
Who knows grace
better than the man
who once denied
and was still embraced?
I close this letter,
grateful that even those
who stumble
can finish strong.

JOHN, THE OLD MAN, WRITES

By now, he's the last one left.
No more Peter,
no more Paul,
just John, writing
like a grandfather
with a twinkle in his eye
and a heart too full
for anything but love.
No greetings,
no pleasantries—
just straight into it:
God is light.
Walk in it.
Love one another.
Stop pretending you don't sin.
But also—stop making sin your hobby.
His words circle,
spiraling back,
as if he knows
we didn't quite get it
the first time.
Love each other.
Not in theory,
but in real, actual,
hard-to-do ways—
like forgiving,

like giving,
like laying down
whatever you cling to
for the sake of another.
John has no patience
for in-between people—
**You're either in the light
or stumbling in the dark.
You either love
or you don't.
You either have Christ
or you don't.**
And then, as if
he knows how we worry,
he reminds us—
we can know.
We can rest.
We can be confident.
Because in the end,
it's not about
how strong we grip Him,
but how strong
He holds us.
I close this letter,
feeling a little more certain
that love really is
the whole point.

JOHN KEEPS IT SHORT

The old man writes again,
but this time,
he keeps it brief—
like a note left
on the kitchen table.
To the lady and her children,
he says,
which could mean a church,
or a family,
or maybe both.
John has a way
of making things
bigger and smaller
at the same time.
The message?
Same as before—
love one another,
walk in truth,
watch out for liars.
He doesn't like
those traveling teachers
who show up smiling,
but quietly rewrite
the gospel
when no one is looking.

Don't even let them in,
he warns,
as if falsehood
spreads like mold
in a damp house.
Then, almost suddenly,
he stops—
I have more to say,
but I'd rather see you in person.
I close this letter,
wishing more people
wrote like John—
honest, warm,
and just long enough.

JOHN, ONE MORE TIME

John writes again,
this time to Gaius,
whose name sounds
like the kind of person
you'd want to have coffee with—
kind, generous,
the kind of soul
who makes church feel like home.
He thanks him
for his hospitality,
for loving the strangers
who wandered in—
the missionaries,
the teachers,
the ones with no place to stay
except the hearts of people like Gaius.
Then there's Diotrephes—
who's a bit of a troublemaker,
refusing to show hospitality,
even trying to kick people out.
John doesn't mince words:
Don't be like Diotrephes.
Which is fair.
Who wants to be known
for making church harder
than it needs to be?

Finally, he ends with Demetrius—
who sounds like someone
you'd trust with your life,
a man with a good testimony,
a man who walks in truth.
And John, always the grandfather,
sends his love,
promising to visit soon,
though he's probably
already written more than
he meant to.
I close this letter,
glad for Gaius,
hopeful for Demetrius,
and relieved to be
nothing like Diotrephes.

JUDE'S ONE LAST WARNING

Jude, who is somehow
both the brother of James
and the cousin of Jesus,
writes one last letter
before the ink runs out
on his patience.
He starts with a flourish—
To those who are called, beloved,
kept for Jesus Christ.
Which sounds nice,
but also makes me feel
like he's talking to someone else
entirely.
He wants to remind us
that we are meant to fight
for the faith,
as if faith were something
you could put in a box
and carry around,
protecting it
from the wild things
that want to steal it.
Then he takes a sharp turn,
talking about people
who sneak in—
the ones who turn grace
into a free-for-all,

the ones who defile the flesh
while quoting Scripture
as if it were a badge
for their bad behavior.
Jude's not having it.
He calls them "clouds without water,"
"autumn trees without fruit,"
"wild waves of the sea"—
a whole buffet of metaphor
for people who are all show
and no substance.
Then, like a good poet,
he throws in a strange warning
about Michael the archangel
and a dispute over the body of Moses—
because, sure,
why not?
Finally, Jude ends with a doxology,
one last prayer:
Now to him who is able
to keep you from stumbling—
which sounds like exactly
what I need to hear,
since I've been tripping
over my own feet
since breakfast.
I close this letter,
wondering if the fight for faith
is less about swinging fists
and more about
staying on your feet
when the world wants you to fall.

REVELATION: THE LAST VISION

John, the last one standing,
the one who heard the voice like a trumpet,
writes down what no one else could,
and we're still trying to figure out
what he saw—
a swirling mix of chaos,
glory, and unthinkable colors
we don't have words for.
A scroll with seven seals,
that no one could open
except the Lamb,
who's not really a lamb
but somehow is.
And don't even get me started
on the scroll that unrolls
into judgment,
the sky darkening
like a bad idea
rolling in.
There are beasts,
like the ones we used to fear in childhood—
except these beasts have horns
and crowns
and a taste for destruction.
And what's with the woman clothed with the sun,
standing on the moon,
with twelve stars in her crown?

Is this a symbol,
or is John just sketching out
the kind of dreams
that make you wonder
what you ate before bed?
The images don't sit still—
they shift, they roar,
they spin like broken mirrors
reflecting pieces of something holy
and terrifying at once.
Four horsemen race across the sky,
their hooves beating
the rhythm of fate—
and the oceans turn to blood,
as if the world was just too full
of stories to handle.
And through it all,
God stands.
Or is He sitting?
Or is He both?
I'm not sure.
But I think John is trying
to show us that
ultimate reality
isn't what we think it is.
It's like John took
the most colorful,
most explosive bits
of what he was allowed to see,
and he painted a portrait of truth
that's somehow distorted—

as if the canvas itself
couldn't hold what was too big
for our understanding.
But in the end,
the new heaven,
the new earth—
there's no more pain,
no more death,
and the Lamb,
who isn't quite a lamb,
is with us,
and the tears are wiped away.
I close this letter,
wondering if John was just
trying to catch a glimpse
of what's too vast for us—
a portrait painted
with words
and flashes of light,
forever unfinished
but somehow still complete.

Epilogue

THESE POEMS WERE NOT written in a rush nor were they completed in a single sitting. They took years to write, each one following the slow, deliberate process of reading, reflecting, and, at times, wrestling with the words of Scripture. It was not a quick project, but rather a steady unfolding of thoughts and feelings after I finished each book of the Bible. There's a rhythm to this work, a slow burn of curiosity that didn't let go. I would finish one book, let it sit with me for a while, then write the poem when the words had time to settle—sometimes just a few weeks, sometimes much longer.

Each poem came from my reflections, the pieces of the text that stood out to me or challenged me in unexpected ways. Some were humorous because the Bible—despite its lofty and eternal themes—often leaves me in awe of how wonderfully strange it is. Other times, the verses felt like a weight on my chest, something to wrestle with or question. But through all of it, my aim was to hold these ancient words up to the light, turning them like a jewel, noticing their edges, their brilliance, their shadows.

Some poems came in bursts of energy, while others took their time, twisting and turning as I tried to understand the deeper things of God. And with every poem, I had one simple hope: that these reflections would speak to you, too, as you put down each book or letter, having read the words that once felt distant but now sit a little closer.

In the end, I hope these poems serve as a gentle invitation to look again—perhaps with humor, perhaps with wonder, perhaps

Epilogue

with challenge—at the Scriptures we hold so dear. These poems are my humble attempt to bridge the gap between the ancient text and my own world, my own life, my own questions. And maybe, just maybe, they have helped you see the Bible a little differently, as it invites you to pause, reflect, and find meaning in the everyday miracles of the Word.

I close this book,
but not the journey.
—Zac

Index of Verses Referenced

PART 1

Genesis

- 1:1—"In the beginning God created the heavens and the earth."
- 12:1-3—"The LORD had said to Abram, 'Go from your country, your people and your father's household to the land I will show you.'"
- 22:1-18—The story of Abraham's faith and God's provision of the ram.

Exodus

- 3:14—"God said to Moses, 'I AM WHO I AM.'"
- 14:21-22—"Then Moses stretched out his hand over the sea, and all that night the LORD drove the sea back with a strong east wind and turned it into dry land."

Leviticus

- 11:44-45—"I am the LORD your God; consecrate yourselves and be holy, because I am holy."

Index of Verses Referenced

- 19:18—"Love your neighbor as yourself."

Numbers

- 6:24-26—"The LORD bless you and keep you; the LORD make his face shine on you and be gracious to you."

Deuteronomy

- 6:4-5—"Hear, O Israel: The LORD our God, the LORD is one. Love the LORD your God with all your heart and with all your soul and with all your strength."
- 31:6—"Be strong and courageous. Do not be afraid or terrified because of them, for the LORD your God goes with you; he will never leave you nor forsake you."

Joshua

- 1:9—"Have I not commanded you? Be strong and courageous. Do not be afraid; do not be discouraged, for the LORD your God will be with you wherever you go."

Judges

- 17:6—"In those days Israel had no king; everyone did as they saw fit."
- 21:25—"In those days Israel had no king; everyone did as they saw fit."

Ruth

- 1:16—"Where you go, I will go, and where you stay, I will stay. Your people will be my people and your God my God."

Index of Verses Referenced

1 Samuel

- 16:7—"The LORD does not look at the things people look at. People look at the outward appearance, but the LORD looks at the heart."

2 Samuel

- 7:12–16—"When your days are over and you rest with your ancestors, I will raise up your offspring to succeed you, your own flesh and blood, and I will establish his kingdom."

1 Kings

- 3:9—"So give your servant a discerning heart to govern your people and to distinguish between right and wrong."
- 19:12—"After the earthquake came a fire, but the LORD was not in the fire. And after the fire came a gentle whisper."

2 Kings

- 2:11—"As they were walking along and talking together, suddenly a chariot of fire and horses of fire appeared and separated the two of them, and Elijah went up to heaven in a whirlwind."

1 Chronicles

- 16:34—"Give thanks to the LORD, for he is good; his love endures forever."
- 28:9—"And you, my son Solomon, acknowledge the God of your father, and serve him with wholehearted devotion and with a willing mind."

Index of Verses Referenced

2 Chronicles

- 7:14—"If my people, who are called by my name, will humble themselves and pray and seek my face and turn from their wicked ways, then I will hear from heaven."

Ezra

- 3:10—"When the builders laid the foundation of the temple of the LORD, the priests in their vestments and with trumpets, and the Levites (the sons of Asaph) with cymbals, took their places to praise the LORD."

Nehemiah

- 8:10—"Nehemiah said, 'Go and enjoy choice food and sweet drinks, and send some to those who have nothing prepared. This day is sacred to our Lord. Do not grieve, for the joy of the LORD is your strength.'"

Esther

- 4:14—"And who knows but that you have come to your royal position for such a time as this?"

Job

- 1:21—"The LORD gave and the LORD has taken away; may the name of the LORD be praised."
- 42:5–6—"My ears had heard of you, but now my eyes have seen you. Therefore I despise myself and repent in dust and ashes."

Index of Verses Referenced

Psalms

- 23:1—"The LORD is my shepherd, I lack nothing."
- 46:1—"God is our refuge and strength, an ever-present help in trouble."
- 150:6—"Let everything that has breath praise the LORD."

Proverbs

- 3:5-6—"Trust in the LORD with all your heart and lean not on your own understanding; in all your ways submit to him, and he will make your paths straight."
- 4:23—"Above all else, guard your heart, for everything you do flows from it."

Ecclesiastes

- 3:1—"There is a time for everything, and a season for every activity under the heavens."
- 12:13—"Now all has been heard; here is the conclusion of the matter: Fear God and keep his commandments, for this is the duty of all mankind."

Song of Songs

- 2:16—"My beloved is mine and I am his; he browses among the lilies."

Isaiah

- 9:6—"For to us a child is born, to us a son is given, and the government will be on his shoulders."

Index of Verses Referenced

- 55:8–9—"'For my thoughts are not your thoughts, neither are your ways my ways,' declares the LORD."

Jeremiah

- 29:11—"'For I know the plans I have for you,' declares the LORD, 'plans for welfare and not for evil, to give you a future and a hope.'"

Lamentations

- 3:22–23—"Because of the LORD's great love we are not consumed, for his compassions never fail. They are new every morning; great is your faithfulness."

Ezekiel

- 37:1–10—The vision of the dry bones coming to life.
- 36:26—"I will give you a new heart and put a new spirit in you; I will remove from you your heart of stone and give you a heart of flesh."

Daniel

- 3:16–18—"Shadrach, Meshach, and Abednego replied to him, 'King Nebuchadnezzar, we do not need to defend ourselves before you in this matter.'"
- 12:3—"Those who are wise will shine like the brightness of the heavens, and those who lead many to righteousness, like the stars for ever and ever."

Index of Verses Referenced

Hosea

- 2:19–20—"I will betroth you to me forever; I will betroth you in righteousness and justice, in love and compassion."

Joel

- 2:28—"And afterward, I will pour out my Spirit on all people. Your sons and daughters will prophesy, your old men will dream dreams, your young men will see visions."

Amos

- 5:24—"But let justice roll on like a river, righteousness like a never-failing stream!"

Obadiah

- 1:15—"The day of the LORD is near for all nations. As you have done, it will be done to you; your deeds will return upon your own head."

Jonah

- 4:11—"And should I not have concern for the great city of Nineveh, in which there are more than a hundred and twenty thousand people . . . ?"

Micah

- 6:8—"He has shown you, O mortal, what is good. And what does the LORD require of you? To act justly and to love mercy and to walk humbly with your God."

Index of Verses Referenced

Nahum

- 1:7—"The LORD is good, a refuge in times of trouble. He cares for those who trust in him."

Habakkuk

- 2:4—"The righteous person will live by his faithfulness."
- 3:17–19—"Though the fig tree does not bud and there are no grapes on the vines . . ."

Zephaniah

- 3:17—"The LORD your God is with you, the Mighty Warrior who saves. He will take great delight in you; in his love he will no longer rebuke you, but will rejoice over you with singing."

Haggai

- 2:9—"The glory of this present house will be greater than the glory of the former house."

Zechariah

- 4:6—"'Not by might nor by power, but by my Spirit,' says the LORD Almighty."

Malachi

- 3:1—"I will send my messenger, who will prepare the way before me."
- 4:2—"But for you who revere my name, the sun of righteousness will rise with healing in its rays."

INDEX OF VERSES REFERENCED

PART 2

Matthew

- 5:14-16—"You are the light of the world. A town built on a hill cannot be hidden."
- 11:28-30—"Come to me, all you who are weary and burdened, and I will give you rest."
- 28:18-20—"Therefore go and make disciples of all nations, baptizing them in the name of the Father and of the Son and of the Holy Spirit."

Mark

- 4:39—"He got up, rebuked the wind and said to the waves, 'Quiet! Be still!'"
- 9:24—"I do believe; help me overcome my unbelief!"
- 10:14—"Let the little children come to me, and do not hinder them, for the kingdom of God belongs to such as these."

Luke

- 1:37—"For no word from God will ever fail."
- 6:27-28—"But to you who are listening I say: Love your enemies, do good to those who hate you."
- 15:11-32—The parable of the prodigal son.

John

- 1:14—"The Word became flesh and made his dwelling among us."

Index of Verses Referenced

- 3:16—"For God so loved the world that he gave his one and only Son, that whoever believes in him shall not perish but have eternal life."
- 20:29—"Then Jesus told him, 'Because you have seen me, you have believed; blessed are those who have not seen and yet have believed.'"

Acts

- 2:42-47—"They devoted themselves to the apostles' teaching and to fellowship, to the breaking of bread and to prayer."
- 4:32-35—"All the believers were one in heart and mind. No one claimed that any of their possessions was their own, but they shared everything they had."
- 16:31—"They replied, 'Believe in the Lord Jesus, and you will be saved—you and your household.'"

Romans

- 3:23—"For all have sinned and fall short of the glory of God."
- 8:28—"And we know that in all things God works for the good of those who love him, who have been called according to his purpose."
- 12:2—"Do not conform to the pattern of this world, but be transformed by the renewing of your mind."

1 Corinthians

- 13:4-7—"Love is patient, love is kind. It does not envy, it does not boast, it is not proud."
- 10:13—"No temptation has overtaken you except what is common to mankind. And God is faithful; he will not let you be tempted beyond what you can bear."

- 15:58—"Therefore, my dear brothers and sisters, stand firm. Let nothing move you. Always give yourselves fully to the work of the Lord."

2 Corinthians

- 4:7—"But we have this treasure in jars of clay to show that this all-surpassing power is from God and not from us."
- 5:17—"Therefore, if anyone is in Christ, the new creation has come: The old has gone, the new is here!"
- 12:9—"But he said to me, 'My grace is sufficient for you, for my power is made perfect in weakness.'"

Galatians

- 5:22-23—"But the fruit of the Spirit is love, joy, peace, forbearance, kindness, goodness, faithfulness, gentleness and self-control."
- 6:9—"Let us not become weary in doing good, for at the proper time we will reap a harvest if we do not give up."

Ephesians

- 2:8-9—"For it is by grace you have been saved, through faith—and this is not from yourselves, it is the gift of God—not by works, so that no one can boast."
- 6:10-18—The armor of God.
- 5:8—"For you were once darkness, but now you are light in the Lord. Live as children of light."

Index of Verses Referenced

Philippians

- 1:6—"Being confident of this, that he who began a good work in you will carry it on to completion until the day of Christ Jesus."
- 4:4–7—"Rejoice in the Lord always. I will say it again: Rejoice! Let your gentleness be evident to all."
- 4:13—"I can do all this through him who gives me strength."

Colossians

- 1:16–17—"For in him all things were created: things in heaven and on earth, visible and invisible."
- 3:23–24—"Whatever you do, work at it with all your heart, as working for the Lord, not for human masters."
- 3:12–14—"Therefore, as God's chosen people, holy and dearly loved, clothe yourselves with compassion, kindness, humility, gentleness and patience."

1 Thessalonians

- 5:16–18—"Rejoice always, pray continually, give thanks in all circumstances."
- 4:16–18—"For the Lord himself will come down from heaven, with a loud command, with the voice of the archangel."

2 Thessalonians

- 3:3—"But the Lord is faithful, and he will strengthen you and protect you from the evil one."

Index of Verses Referenced

1 Timothy

- 1:15—"Here is a trustworthy saying that deserves full acceptance: Christ Jesus came into the world to save sinners—of whom I am the worst."
- 6:12—"Fight the good fight of the faith. Take hold of the eternal life to which you were called when you made your good confession."

2 Timothy

- 1:7—"For the Spirit God gave us does not make us timid, but gives us power, love and self-discipline."
- 4:7-8—"I have fought the good fight, I have finished the race, I have kept the faith."

Titus

- 2:11-12—"For the grace of God has appeared that offers salvation to all people. It teaches us to say 'No' to ungodliness."

Philemon

- 1:15-16—"Perhaps the reason he was separated from you for a little while was that you might have him back forever—no longer as a slave, but better than a slave, as a dear brother."

Hebrews

- 4:12—"For the word of God is alive and active. Sharper than any double-edged sword."
- 12:1-2—"Therefore, since we are surrounded by such a great cloud of witnesses, let us throw off everything that hinders."

Index of Verses Referenced

James

- 1:2–4—"Consider it pure joy, my brothers and sisters, whenever you face trials of many kinds."
- 2:17—"In the same way, faith by itself, if it is not accompanied by action, is dead."
- 4:10—"Humble yourselves before the Lord, and he will lift you up."

1 Peter

- 1:3–4—"Praise be to the God and Father of our Lord Jesus Christ! In his great mercy he has given us new birth into a living hope."
- 5:7—"Cast all your anxiety on him because he cares for you."

2 Peter

- 1:3–4—"His divine power has given us everything we need for a godly life."

1 John

- 1:5—"This is the message we have heard from him and declare to you: God is light; in him there is no darkness at all."
- 4:16—"So we have come to know and to believe the love that God has for us. God is love."

2 John

- 1:6—"And this is love: that we walk in obedience to his commands."

Index of Verses Referenced

3 John

- 1:4—"I have no greater joy than to hear that my children are walking in the truth."

Jude

- 1:24-25—"To him who is able to keep you from stumbling and to present you before his glorious presence without fault..."

Revelation

- 1:7—"Look, he is coming with the clouds, and every eye will see him."
- 7:17—"For the Lamb at the center of the throne will be their shepherd."
- 21:1-4—"Then I saw 'a new heaven and a new earth,' for the first heaven and the first earth had passed away."

www.ingramcontent.com/pod-product-compliance
Lightning Source LLC
Chambersburg PA
CBHW050800160426
43192CB00010B/1584